Advance Praise for *Searching for the Sacred*

As soon as I read a dozen or so of these devotionals, I knew what I wanted to do: go back to the beginning, slow down, savor one each day, and then, after two months, start over again. Rev. Cameron Trimble's insights are rich, poignant, and on point ... and they will help you search each day for the sacred in your daily experience.

— Brian D. McLaren, Author, *Do I Stay Christian?*

In this troubling, exhausting time of life, Cameron Trimble gently draws us back to the deep waters of rest. Her insight inspires us to take a simple, small moment. In doing so, we find we are ready once more for the challenging moment at our door.

— Rev. Dr. Jacqui Lewis, Public Theologian, Activist, and Author, *Fierce Love: A bold path to ferocious courage and rule-breaking kindness that can heal the world*

Cameron's words are good medicine for weary souls in need of relief. These reflections are a clear and beautiful reminder that for those who move through this world in love, the ground we are standing on is always holy.

— John Pavlovitz, Author, *A Bigger Table* and *If God is Love, Don't Be a Jerk*

Cameron Trimble is highly regarded for her advice on church leadership in a changing world. With *Searching for the Sacred*, Cameron establishes herself as a reliable guide for any of us who seek to find meaning and purpose in the midst of today's turbulence and chaos. Leaving behind the doctrine and dogma that often plagues devotional works, Cameron presents a series of brief but compelling stories from her life and that of others to reveal a hidden holiness residing within the holy-mess of modern experience. She shows us how to be wise, deeply present, and kind, in a world that can seem anything but.

— Eric Elnes, Author, *Gifts of the Dark Wood: Seven Blessings for Soulful Skeptics (and Other Wanderers)*

Cameron Trimble's relentlessly faithful reflections will ignite the courage needed to engage the greatest moral challenges humanity has ever faced.

— Rev. Dr. Jim Antal, Special Advisor on Climate Justice to UCC General Minister and President

Searching for the Sacred is a poignant series of meditations that meets our current moment. Through reflecting on scripture and other sacred stories, Trimble invites us to go deeper into our spiritual practices to find healing, transformation, renewal, connection and courage to see the new thing God is doing in this season.

— Rev. Jennifer Butler, Founder in Residence, Faith in Public Life

Cameron's sensitivity to modern mythos, her imaginative use of metaphor, and her grounded spirituality make this devotional book both very readable and deeply insightful. She has become one of my trusted spiritual guides. She makes the sacred accessible.

— Rev. Dr. John Dorhauer, General Minister and President, United Church of Christ

Rev. Trimble clearly reads...everything. In this collection, she distills the breadth of her wisdom so that, in daily practice, our own faith can take flight. This writingA is a joy to behold. I didn't want it to end!

— Rev. Kaji S. Douša, Senior Pastor, Park Avenue Christian Church

In these pages, Rev. Cameron Trimble scans her life and focuses on a wisdom-producing moment. As I read and reflected, those crucial points in time transformed me.

— Rev. Carol Howard Merritt, Pastor and Author, *Healing Spiritual Wounds*

What a timely and so needed offering! As we reel from the devastation of climate change, the violence of hate, greed and the general failure of human community to hold our children and youth in all their diversity, *Searching for the Sacred* offers us both a home for the heart and a path forward. If we cannot change the world ourselves, we *can* allow ourselves to be changed by the practices and stories in this book, and that changes everything. Evocative, practical, wise, real and a means to that sacred connection that is the source of abundance in our life together. Please give it a 60 day try, for all our sakes.

— Robert G. Dalgleish, Founding Director, Edge Network, The United Church of Canada

Searching for the Sacred

Sixty Meditations on Faith, Hope, & Love

Cameron Trimble

Saint Louis, Missouri

An imprint of Christian Board of Publication

Print ISBN 97808272031894
EPUB 9780827231900
EPDF 9780827231917

ChalicePress.com

Printed in Canada

Contents

To Rev. Dr. James McCormick,
who taught me to love

good theology,
big questions,
and resilient hope.

Introduction

You may have picked up this book simply because you were looking for a new devotional to start or end your day. Perhaps the title or the cover grabbed you. Wonderful! I hope you find in this book stories and parables that give you hope, insight, courage, and resilience.

You might also have picked up this book because you have a sense, as I do, that we are living between times. Something is at stake in our evolution, in our awakening, as never before. We are living at the end of one era and the beginning of another, one marked by some of the greatest challenges humankind has ever faced. We walk into a future shaped by global warming, mass migration, the extinction of millions of species, political unrest, the acceleration of technology, the globalization of economies, and the unweaving of institutions that have shaped our lives for generations.

But we also walk into a future open to a new kind of spiritual consciousness, an awakening to our interdependence with one another and all of creation. That connection, which has always been present, now invites each of us to imagine the world we could build together should we have the will and the courage to do so. Ours is an era of unprecedented change, the most radical deconstruction and reconstruction the world has ever seen. We need a new mind, a new way of seeing, if we are to chart a generative path forward for our future generations.

So, you see, by reading this book of meditations, we are up to something together. We are living in mythic times. We are living within the tension of deep awakening and deep, willful blindness. We are between stories. We are deciding whether ours will be the story of the Great Turning, when we honor our interdependence with creation and embrace ways to live sustainably on the earth. Or will we miss the moment, the time we could have saved ourselves and our children, but could not muster the wisdom or the will to do so?

What story will we live? Philosopher and author Jean Houston once said, "We are 'mything links,' links between the great mythic stories, the great stories of all times and places, and the playing out of those stories in everyday life." How we live out those linkages determines a great deal at this point, so it is important that we are aware of the world we create.

Surely there are many ways to develop our spiritual consciousness. Why invest time in a book of meditations? In my life as a pastor, I appreciate how rituals and reflection work together to deepen our senses and our sense of self. A daily practice of reading, reflecting, and journaling can have a powerful effect on how we perceive "what is so" in our world and where God might be leading us to make a difference.

The lessons I have learned as a pilot are woven throughout this book as they have been great teachers for me. Changes in altitude grant us different ways of seeing the world that create new possibilities for acting. At the same time, forces like wind gusts, weather fronts, temperature, and air density—all outside of our control—require agile adaptation and change how we fly moment by moment. Safety checks and emergency procedures keep us as safe as possible but can't predict or prevent everything. I've learned that thoughtful attention and daily practice—a theme that I invite throughout this book—have created a muscle memory that makes me a safer pilot. This is how faith works as well. It is something you practice and, in that practice, it both teaches and changes you.

In *Searching for the Sacred*, we will journey together as we seek different altitudes and bring thoughtful attention to our lives. We share a call to rise to this historic moment, to deepen our wisdom and discover how we and God might create a better, more just world for all. I am honored to be on this journey with you.

How to Use This Book

Most of us read devotional books as a way of connecting to an ongoing conversation between ourselves and God. We use the prompts as a threshold, an invitation, to our own listening for God's "still, small voice" in our lives. I encourage you to read these meditations and then simply sit with them. Listen to your own intuition and open yourself to sensing God within you.

This book contains sixty meditations with scripture references and reflection questions. You can start reading at any time of the year. I recommend you read one reflection a day for sixty days, taking time to journal and consider the insights each meditation offers to you. We've left space in the book for you to write, though you might also wish to keep your own journal for longer reflections. You should plan to set aside thirty minutes a day for this practice.

Each meditation begins with a scripture reference from the New Revised Standard Version (NRSV) of the Protestant Bible. This translation, published in 1989, benefits from hundreds of years of biblical scholarship and is considered by most biblical scholars to be the most accurate English translation to date. I hope you will also find that this translation has retained much of the beautiful prose and poetry of the English language without sacrificing the accuracy of the original texts.

If you are a member of a congregation, you may also find this book useful for classes or small group gatherings. Many groups read a meditation together and then use the reflection questions at the end of each chapter to guide their conversations.

I hope you find within the book an invitation to deepen your connection to Love. I hope as you read these meditations, you find yourself becoming more kind, compassionate, and understanding. I hope you sense your connection to all of creation—your interdependence with all that is—and this wakes you to the urgency of acting in this moment to heal our planet and ourselves.

Thank you for taking the time to journey with me through these sixty meditations.

In Prayer

May you live in this truth:
God beneath you,
God in front of you,
God behind you,
God above you,
God within you.

May this truth grant you peace.

Amen.

Meditations

Take Only What You Need

For surely I know the plans I have for you, says the Lord, plans for your welfare and not for harm, to give you a future with hope. (Jeremiah 29:11)

• • •

Recently I had a beautiful conversation with a colleague. Her mother had passed away, and she faced the overwhelming task of cleaning out her home. Weeks passed as she faced the grief she knew this would bring and wrestled with the best way to approach the work.

By a stroke of providence, she connected with a woman who ran an estate sales company. In conversation with her, the woman said to her, "Go through the house and take only what you want. Take all the time you need. Then leave the rest to us. We will take care of it."

As my colleague reflected on that moment, she said, "Her saying those words to me was the most wonderful act of grace. I felt such relief. It allowed me to grieve my mother without the burden of the rest."

As I listened to her story, I thought about so many of us working in companies and faith communities that have been forever changed by the pandemic. So much of our life wasn't working. Companies were forcing too many of us into gray cubicles with mindless work. Our economies were consuming our planet. Faith communities were facing unsustainable financial realities. We were killing ourselves with over-scheduled lives.

It's as if this global disruption was saying to us, "It is time for your old life to die and a new life to be born. Take a moment and look around. Take with you only what you really want and think you will need. Leave everything else. From dust, to dust. All will be cared for."

If you are worried about how to help people through this time, perhaps offer a word about the peace that comes with letting go, taking only what you need. The pattern of life has always been life, death, and life again. We will carry on, lighter and less burdened for the journey ahead. We will thrive.

If you are a leader in a faith community, perhaps consider that this is the "Great Rummage Sale" that our beloved Phyllis Tickle talked about so often. Your work is to let go of the trappings of the institutions that will not serve the movement going forward. Whatever isn't working, whatever you don't want or need, leave behind. This is no time for nostalgia. Our world needs new experiences of sacred awakening. Bring from our traditions only that which draws us into deeper connection to God.

Life is, in the end, about learning when to hold on and when to let go.

Reflection Question

- What parts of your life and self do you want to leave behind in our pre-pandemic world?
- What values and practices do you want to take into the future?

Leave behind worry and move forward
acceptance
Focus on what we have as being enough
Leave behind attachment to things -
even ones that have a history or
familial connection
move forward with assurance God's
promises are true today

An Unexpected Emergency in Flight

Be strong and courageous; do not be frightened or dismayed, for the Lord your God is with you wherever you go. (Joshua 1:9)

• • •

As I was taking off from Peachtree-Dekalb Airport (KPDK) in Atlanta, another pilot who had been cleared to land lowered his landing gear on his dissent as he had hundreds of times before. But this time, as his landing gear descended, it began making a horrible shaking noise. This is never good. He called the tower and reported that he might have an emergency on his hands. All of us in flight immediately tuned in.

The controller called back to the pilot and recommended he do a flyby so that the controllers in the tower, using binoculars, could visually confirm that the landing gear was down. They would not be able to confirm that the landing gear was locked in place, which left the risk open that the gear could collapse once the plane touched the runway. But it's what they could do in the moment. The pilot flew low straight down runway 3L, and the controllers called back, confirming that they could indeed see all three wheels.

They cleared the pilot to circle the airport. The air traffic controller called him, saying, "Our longest runway is yours. When you are ready, and only when you are ready, you are cleared to make your turn and land. We are prepared for you."

He made a wide circle so that he had time to get himself mentally prepared for potential emergency procedures. Ground services and the fire department got in position to meet the plane quickly if his landing gear collapsed. Everything was in place. The rest of us listened (and prayed). We only made radio calls as required by regulation. We wanted to make sure that frequency was open for that pilot to use in any way he needed. The waiting was interminable.

Finally, the pilot entered his final approach. Responding to the air traffic controller, he confirmed there was one soul on board and forty gallons of remaining fuel, which the fire department would need to know to gauge the intensity of the potential emergency.

In this situation, pilots are trained to land the airplane at the lowest speed possible and hold the airplane's weight off the disabled wheel for as long as possible. At some point, gravity takes over, and there's nothing left to be done.

The pilot lined up for runway 3R. He lowered his airspeed to just above stall speed, and then he gently, as if like a feather, placed that airplane onto the runway. The landing gear screeched and shimmied and left black rubber tire marks down the runway. But it remained intact, and he was safe. The controller came back on the radio with his call sign confirming that the plane was clear of the runway. Then he said to the pilot, "Really great job, sir." It was a simple salute that held a universe of relief and respect from all of us.

Things go wrong in life despite our every attempt to make it safe and predictable. We can't anticipate the curveballs that life throws our way even as we try to prepare to handle them in the safest way possible. Life is risky. The wondrous gift is that as we each experience our moments of challenge, we are never alone.

Compassion is the comforting presence we grant one another in the moments of our deep challenges. It is how we embody the Divine. In that space of loving witness, we meet God in each other and are moved to care for one another's plight.

I often sign my emails and notes with the words, "We are in this together." Yesterday, I was reminded by an ATC controller and a lucky pilot just how essential that truth is.

Reflection Questions

- What curveballs have come your way that felt overwhelming but worked out in the end? What did you learn about yourself?

- Asking for help can be hard. Whose help do you need in your life and what stops you from asking? What if you reached out to them today?

In the Face of Heartbreak and Hope

And the peace of God, which surpasses all understanding, will guard your hearts and your minds in Christ Jesus. (Philippians 4:7)

• • •

Some years ago, I had the chance to visit Israel. We toured the entire country, studying archaeology, learning about the history, and seeing firsthand the strain of so many years of conflict and violence. We met many people whose stories of loss, pain, hope, and faith will stay with me for a lifetime.

One woman I met changed my view of life.

She was an old woman when I met her in the old city of Jerusalem. She made stoles for a living. As I was browsing through her store, I asked her how she started making them, supposing that she was some poor woman who spotted a niche in selling stoles to American pastors who are always looking for some good "bling" for their robes.

Instead, she told me about her life. Many years before, her three children had been with her in the market one day and had the bad luck of being too close to a suicide bomber. She was off buying some vegetables for their dinner that evening when she heard someone scream. She looked back just in time to watch as her children—her life—were blown from the face of the earth. Can you imagine this horror? Can you imagine the sheer unspeaking, crushing pain of this?

She spent the next year of her life in a numb fog, trying to understand how and why this could happen. Until finally, she stopped. She awoke one morning realizing that there are no good answers to these questions. What would answers bring her anyway? What she had to do was to decide how to live.

Her way of living in the midst of her woundedness was to start making these stoles. To her, they became signs of peace and symbols of God's unfailing love. She has a vision of clergy all across the world wearing them as they stand in pulpits, march in protests, and sit with the sick. In her brokenness, she turned to love, gifting us all with her testimony, her handmade art, and her unfailing grace.

When I found the stole I wanted to buy, she placed it over my shoulders. Looking me in the eyes, she said, "This is a symbol of peace that I give to you this day. May every day of your life bring peace to our earth and love to all people." It was the most powerful commissioning I have ever known.

Were I to suffer such terrible loss in my life, I pray that I would have the faith and strength that she has. She could have become deeply bitter. She could have sought revenge. She could have lived with biting anger. But instead, she decided to live believing that God is love and grace is true.

I don't know her name. I wish I did. But when I put on that stole, I give thanks that by grace her life touched mine.

How are you turning your wounds into signs of grace? I think, in the end, that is what Love is finally about.

Reflection Questions

- What has pain taught you about love?
- Bad things happen in life. How does that change how you think about and relate to God?

We Are All One

"I am the Alpha and the Omega," says the Lord God, who is and who was and who is to come, the Almighty. (Revelation 1:8)

• • •

Years ago, I went hiking through the rainforests of Costa Rica. I had never before experienced the magnificent energy of a rainforest. I remember my sense of wonder, walking under a fern frond and looking up to see that fern was nearly twice as tall as me. I brushed plants that recoiled at my touch and then opened again once I passed. I met a lizard braced on a towering tree who looked me straight in the eyes as if to have a conversation with me. Like Alice in Wonderland, I was in awe.

Likely because of that sense of awe, I had my first formative experience of Oneness. In my wonder, something in me shifted just enough for me to grasp an overwhelming sense of interdependence with everything around me. I was me, but I was also the giant fern, grasping plants, towering tree, and talkative lizard. They were also me. I was solid in form, but I also could permeate everything around me, just as everything around me could permeate me.

It's strange to "language" the experience. Mystics talk about "non-dual actualization." The best I can say is that in that moment, and in many since, I have understood at a deep, expansive level that we are all One. We are all stardust, energy flows, Love's greatest expressions. This capacity for non-dual expansion of consciousness is not necessarily unique. It is something that happens to and for many of us, sometimes spontaneously and often through practice. Meditation and prayer have become profound teachers for me for this reason. They are the pathways by which I remember who I am.

As I think about the world we are creating together, I have a growing sense of urgency that our only sustainable future begins with our willingness to ground ourselves (literally) in our awareness of interdependence (Oneness), and then to create our businesses, institutions, politics, and rituals from that fertile soil. Nothing else will hold together the global future that awaits us.

During the Christian season of Advent, we travel through the four themes of hope, peace, joy, and love. We are waiting for God to breakthrough to us. We are waiting to see what has been true all along—our longing to experience hope, peace, joy, and love is actually some wiser part of us calling us to break out of the delusion of dualism. We are not separate from each other nor the planet. We are more connected than we ever dreamed.

Perhaps this sounds crazy to you. If you are willing to risk it, here is my invitation: Get up earlier in the morning than usual. In a quiet space, perhaps after lighting a candle and taking a few deep breaths, repeat this prayer as a mantra, a guide to ease you into openness. When you are there, let it go, and simply . . . be.

Be still and know that I am God.
Be still and know that I am.
Be still and know.
Be still.
Be.

I am praying for you and inspired by who you are becoming. Indeed, the whole future of the world depends on it.

Reflection Questions

- We must move beyond the illusion of separation in order to fully actualize a more holistic vision of our world. How might you explore opening yourself to your interdependence with all of creation?

- Meditation can be challenging for a lot of us. What gets in your way?

In Prayer

May you trust the Great Spirit

who has loved you,

loves you now,

and will always love you,

to guide your steps in these unfolding days.

Amen.

Becoming Real

Who is wise and understanding among you? Show by your good life that your works are done with gentleness born of wisdom. (James 3:13)

• • •

I have felt echoes of my theological training in my exploration of social transformation and transpersonal psychology. It seems that the approaches of human development, psychology, and spirituality all suggest that over time we grow in awareness and awakening. These approaches suggest that we move from a dualist mindset (the world is about me vs. you) to one of interdependence and unity (the world is about all of creation). We move from the illusion of separation to the recognition that all in the universe are united in God.

The way we know we are on that path is by observing a shift in ourselves. We stop defending our "rightness" and start forgiving those who are at earlier stages of understanding. We forgive because we too went through less advanced stages, and we recognize ourselves in them.

For most of us, some form of suffering, loss, failure, or darkness leads us into deeper awareness and growth. Very little of institutional religion is honest about this. In fact, it is the mystics and the outcasts who are undefended enough to pretend that it is otherwise. Mystics teach us that periods of disorientation and confusion where we struggle with our own shadows and failures are core to the human experience. It's our willingness to become REAL that marks the transformation of our journeys.

Margery Williams Bianco writes beautifully about this in her children's book, *The Velveteen Rabbit*. When the young Rabbit asks the old Skin Horse about how to become real, he responds:

> "Real isn't how you are made," said the Skin Horse. "It's a thing that happens to you. When a child loves you for a long, long time, not just to play with, but REALLY loves you, then you become Real."

> "Does it hurt?" asked the Rabbit.
>
> "Sometimes," said the Skin Horse, for he was always truthful. "When you are Real you don't mind being hurt."
>
> "Does it happen all at once, like being wound up," he asked, "or bit by bit?"
>
> "It doesn't happen all at once,"' said the Skin Horse. "You become. It takes a long time. That's why it doesn't happen often to people who break easily, or have sharp edges, or who have to be carefully kept. Generally, by the time you are Real, most of your hair has been loved off, and your eyes drop out and you get loose in the joints and very shabby. But these things don't matter at all, because once you are Real you can't be ugly, except to people who don't understand."

Becoming "real" may make us seem strange, ridiculous, heretical, iconoclastic, and even dangerous to others. But in truth, denying the sacred journey toward wholeness is the real danger.

Reflection Questions

- As you look back over your life, in what moments did you sense you were "becoming real"? When did you sense you were maturing in wisdom?

- Think of a time when you felt completely connected to everything around you. What did you learn from that experience?

Searching for Hope

God said, "This is the sign of the covenant that I make between me and you and every living creature that is with you, for all future generations: I have set my bow in the clouds, and it shall be a sign of the covenant between me and the earth." (Genesis 9:12-13)

• • •

Rainbows always give me hope. In the Old Testament, when Noah saw the rainbow in the sky after the Great Flood, it was the sign that it was safe to emerge from the ark. But it was also a sign that the old world, the only world he had ever known, had been washed away. He would be walking out into a new world that he didn't know. All of the mess of the old world was gone, and the future that was now possible was yet to be revealed. In this way, the rainbow is a transition point, a doorway to new possibilities.

So many of us are hurting right now. Many of us are struggling with addictions, anxiety, stress, emotional exhaustion, or trauma. It becomes easy to lose hope. It becomes so easy to think we are going to be endlessly stuck in the Great Flood of pain that we are tempted to give up and succumb. I understand that. But it is never true because then a rainbow appears. A doorway of hope opens. A friend shows up. A job comes through. An intervention happens. A person offers forgiveness. A treatment works. An unexpected check comes in the mail. A donation is made. Hope becomes real.

The part you have to be ready for is this: having the courage to say "yes." You have to say "yes" to the new world and the new possibilities, to emerge from the ark of pain and loss, grief and unknowing. No one can take that step for you. It is yours to claim for yourself. It may be the hardest and bravest thing you have ever done.

Here is what I do know: a new and wonderful world awaits us on the other side of pain. God's promise to us was never that we would live lives free of pain. We are free beings and as such are capable of creating great pain for ourselves and others. God values our freedom enough to tolerate our suffering. God's promise was that we would never be alone. God is always there, hoping for our healing and our wholeness.

If you are feeling devastated by the mess of the world or the mess of your life, I hope you will search the skies. The rainbows are there. The new world awaits. You have every reason to hope, as long as you have the courage to say "yes."

Remember you are not alone. You have people who love you and a God who will never give up on you. With that in your favor, your best days are ahead.

Reflection Questions

- What blessings do you need to say "yes" to as you move toward healing?
- What might your life look like if you live as if your best days are ahead?

Forgiveness Is a Good Idea for Others

Be kind to one another, tenderhearted, forgiving one another, as God in Christ has forgiven you. (Ephesians 4:32)

• • •

I've decided that forgiveness is a wonderful idea until we actually have something or someone to forgive. The idea is only slightly better if I am the one who needs to be forgiven.

Each of us has had a moment in life where forgiveness became more than a lesson we learned from sermons or teachers. It became an experience that reshaped us. Saying "I am sorry" (and meaning it) means that you see the harm, the pain, the wrong that you created, and you offer contrition. More than that, you change your ways. Or someone says "I am sorry" to you, and in that act, you release your anger, hurt, and rejection directed toward them.

"I'm sorry" are two of the most important words in the English language. Without this possibility of restoring trust and mending broken fences, the inherently flawed experience of being human would feel impossibly tragic. A good apology is deeply healing, while an absent or bad one can compromise and even end a relationship.

In a *Forbes* interview, Dr. Harriet Lerner, PhD, author of the book *Why Won't You Apologize?: Healing Big Betrayals and Everyday Hurts*, reflects on the impact of forgiveness in leadership:

> Our ability to lead, whether at home or at work, rests on our ability to orient to reality, and to take responsibility for our mistakes, and to apologize for them. The level of respect we earn from others, as well as our own level of maturity, rest squarely on our ability to see ourselves objectively, to take a clear-eyed look at the ways that our behavior affects others, and to be fully accountable for our mistakes without blaming others. The courage to apologize and the wisdom to do it wisely and well is at the heart of friendship, leadership, marriage, parenting and being grounded in maturity, integrity

and self-worth. It's hard to imagine what's more important than that.

Forgiveness is also at the heart of all good religion. For Christians, forgiving one another is not something Jesus asks us to consider; it is something Jesus commands us to do. If we want to live in right relationship with one another, giving and receiving forgiveness is not optional. It is foundational to a faithful life.

We have a great deal in our lives and our world that deserves rejection and correction. Forgiveness is not a substitute for justice. But when we find ourselves separated and divided from those we need and love, we find our way back to one another through the simple act of seeing one another's pain and saying, "I am sorry."

Ephesians 4:32 puts it beautifully: "Be kind to one another, tenderhearted, forgiving one another, as God in Christ has forgiven you." I hope you find freedom today in the giving and receiving of forgiveness. I have come to realize this is the path to peace.

Reflection Questions

- What difference has forgiving others made in your own life?
- Reflect on a time when you needed and were granted forgiveness from someone. How did that change you?

We All Belong

Then God said, "Let us make humankind in our image, according to our likeness; and let them have dominion over the fish of the sea, and over the birds of the air, and over the cattle, and over all the wild animals of the earth, and over every creeping thing that creeps upon the earth." (Genesis 1:26)

• • •

On her podcast, *On Being*, journalist Krista Tippett interviewed astronomer, Dr. Jill Tarter about her work searching for life on other planets. Jill was the inspiration for Dr. Ellie Arroway, played by Jodie Foster in the 1997 movie *Contact*. Tarter has devoted her career to searching for signals sent from technologically advanced cultures on other planets. Yes, it sounds crazy. But if you listen to her explain it, I bet she will convince you that it might be the best job on earth.

During the interview, I was struck by their conversation about thinking of ourselves as "earthlings." While not the first label we think to apply to ourselves, Dr. Tarter suggests that understanding ourselves as earthlings might just save the world. She explains:

> [This cosmic exploration] has the philosophical equivalence of holding up a mirror to every individual on this planet and saying, "See, all of you? You're all the same, when compared to something out there that had evolved independently." And so I really like the potential of SETI [her organization] for changing people's perspective and trivializing the differences among humans—differences that we're so willing to shed blood over when, indeed, we are all human. We are all earthlings. We are all the same, compared to something else. And if you see yourself as an earthling before you see yourself as a Californian, then I think that sets the stage for tackling really difficult challenges on a global scale.

I appreciate Dr. Tarter's imagery inviting us to broaden our vision of connection. She is asking us to see ourselves at the level of earthling—

the label we ALL have in common—to highlight that at that scale, we are more the same than different. Our divisions are useless at that scale. None of us can claim exceptionalism or exclusion. At the scale of the cosmos, we are all earthlings. We all belong to one another.

The global pandemic has also helped us see our interdependence, even as it has laid bare the barriers we create to give us the illusion of separation. But at the scale of the heavens, we are all part of one tribe. We all belong. We are all One.

Today, I invite us to hold the idea that 13.8 billion years ago, the cosmos birthed us all. We might tell the story this way: God said, "Let us create humans in our own image," and from the stardust of a wild and wonderful cosmic collision, we were born. And God said, "Ah, yes, we shall call them earthlings, because they are ALL made of the stars and hold the beauty of all creation within them." And God looked upon creation and smiled. It was good.

Reflection Questions

- If you think of yourself as an earthling—all of us children of God—does that change how you relate to others?
- Contemplate that you are made of stardust and that you hold the beauty of creation within your being. What shifts within you?

In Prayer

Lord, make me an instrument of your peace.
Where there is hatred, let me bring love.
Where there is offense, let me bring pardon.
Where there is discord, let me bring union.
Where there is error, let me bring truth.
Where there is doubt, let me bring faith.
Where there is despair, let me bring hope.
Where there is darkness, let me bring your light.
Where there is sadness, let me bring joy
O Master, let me not seek as much
to be consoled as to console,
to be understood as to understand,
to be loved as to love,
for it is in giving that one receives,
it is in self-forgetting that one finds,
it is in pardoning that one is pardoned,
it is in dying that one is raised to eternal life.
Prayer of Saint Francis of Assisi

If the Suit Doesn't Fit

> *But the Lord said to Samuel, "Do not look on his appearance or on the height of his stature, because I have rejected him; for the Lord does not see as mortals see; they look on the outward appearance, but the Lord looks on the heart." (1 Samuel 16:7)*

• • •

A fable for our time . . .

Hans, the tailor, was famous through all of the lands for his skill in sewing the perfect suit. Because of his reputation, an influential entrepreneur visiting his city ordered a tailor-made suit. But when he came to pick up his suit, the customer found one sleeve twisted that way and the other this way; one shoulder bulged out, and the other caved in. He tugged and pulled and managed to make his body fit.

As he returned home on the bus, another passenger noticed his odd appearance and asked if Hans, the tailor, made the suit. Receiving an affirmative reply, the man remarked, "Amazing! I knew that Hans was a good tailor, but I had no idea he could make a suit fit so perfectly someone as deformed as you."

We spend a lot of our lives twisting and contorting ourselves into the shape of others' expectations—our parents, boss, spouse, friends, children, and social media feeds. We push and shove ourselves into grotesque configurations until we fit wonderfully into their comfort zones.

At some point, if we are lucky, we stop playing such games. If we are lucky, we grow up and grow into ourselves.

This is the moment of true transformation because only then can we understand the essence of our great faith traditions. At the heart of good religion is this essential truth: we are "fearfully and wonderfully made." We are made in the image of God, beautiful and complete—from the beginning, middle, and end. Our lives are about celebrating that fundamental truth and then living so fully AS OURSELVES that people see God's artistry in and through us.

Today, when you feel your shoulders slump or your neck tighten, curiously explore whether you are contorting yourself for someone else. If your head starts pounding or your stomach clinches, question whether you are disfiguring yourself for approval. If so, simply . . . stop. Stop pretending to be less than who you are meant to be.

If the suit doesn't fit, don't wear it.

Reflection Questions

- Remember a time when you distorted yourself—your commitments, values, behavior—to appease or please someone else. What did that cost you?

- In what ways might you be contorting yourself today?

What a Great Day!

So we have known and believe the love that God has for us. God is love, and those who abide in love abide in God, and God abides in them. (1 John 4:16)

• • •

In the third grade I had the good fortune to befriend a guy named Jesse. Our friendship was accidental; our teacher just happened to assign the two of us to sit next to each other in class. As it turns out, she put two troublemakers next to each other, and we hit it off beautifully.

Jesse was a kind and playful soul who had the misfortune of ending up in a foster care system that had him move dozens of times throughout his childhood. If I had had that experience, I suspect I might become suspicious of people or bitter about my lot in life. But Jesse had a God-given gift of seeing the best in people and believing that ultimately the people in his life were up to good.

In truth, you could argue that Jesse was gullible. When I figured this out, I remember playfully testing my theory. I would say things like, "Jesse, this afternoon the teachers are going to cancel class, and we are going to spend the entire afternoon on the playground." He would say, "Really? Wouldn't that be great? What a great day!" He was so excited. Or I might say, "Jesse, the fire department might come and bring their trucks to the school so that we can play on them." "Oh wow," he would say, "what a great day!" He figured out my game pretty quickly, but still he played along. I came to love this in him, and I wish I had more of it myself.

That summer, Jesse and I ended up at a church camp together. As part of our week there, we had to sit and listen to the pastor give us a LONG sermon on why we should all be Christians. I remember sitting in the hard pew hearing nothing but, "whah, whah, whah." I couldn't wait for it to be over. Then I looked over at Jesse. He was entranced, his eyes locked onto the pastor as he spoke. When the sermon finally ended, and we walked out, I asked Jesse what he heard. He said, *"God loves me! I never knew that. What a great day!"*

Two months later, Jesse didn't come back to school. He moved on to a different school with some other family and some other friends. As I look back at that very special friendship, I give thanks to God for letting me know someone like Jesse. In a moment when my ears were deaf to great news that would change my life, Jesse heard the words of hope.

What a great day!

Reflection Questions

- When did it finally sink in that God loves you? What difference has that made in your life?

- What have your friendships taught you about love, hope, and belonging?

Pivot Points

If we live, we live to the Lord, and if we die, we die to the Lord; so then, whether we live or whether we die, we are the Lord's. (Romans 14:8)

• • •

"I wish I had more control of my life," my friend said. "I feel so anxious. I make decisions constantly in my life, but I have no idea how they will turn out. I wish I could see the future. Life feels so . . . risky."

My friend had just been offered her dream job. She would need to move to a new city. But on the same day, she got a call from her mother telling her she had been diagnosed with a challenging health condition. She was in a tough bind. My friend was facing a "pivot point."

Each of us faces pivot points that suddenly change everything in our lives. Simple phrases redefine our whole reality.

"We are engaged. "
"It's a girl."
"You got the job."
"I want a divorce."
"It's cancer."
"I love you."
"He's gone."
"I'm pregnant."
"Yes."
"No."
"I quit."
"I accept."

We can look back on our lives and see moments where our decisions set us on certain paths that determine the conditions for the next set of decisions. Some of our choices bring us regret and some great joy. All of them teach us.

I understand my friend's yearning for some predictability in life, some assurance that the pivot points lead to happiness rather than regret.

So much of our lives are changing right now. That has always been true, but the safety nets that we use to protect us from the impacts of change are crumbling around us—job security, housing security, health security, family security. Life does indeed feel risky. It's why I am grateful to be a person of faith.

In Romans 14:8 we hear, "If we live, we live to the Lord, and if we die, we die to the Lord; so then, whether we live or whether we die, we are the Lord's." No matter what the "pivot" brings, we are not alone. We are not abandoned. We should not be afraid.

Good theology is rooted in the conviction that, on the whole, all things are at work for our well-being. Of course, that does not mean that bad things don't happen. But I believe that the long arc of the universe bends toward love, justice, healing, and peace. That impulse is built into the very source code of life. While bad things may happen, I trust that the flow of life is ultimately working for the common good.

Futurist and author Octavia Butler reminds us in the novel *The Parable of the Sower*, "All that you touch you Change. All that you Change Changes you. The only lasting truth is Change. God Is Change."

Embrace the pivot—God will meet you there.

Reflection Questions

- What changes in your life today are creating anxiety for you?
- How does Romans 14:8 help reframe change with God?

Dancing with the Shadow

If we live by the Spirit, let us also be guided by the Spirit. Let us not become conceited, competing against one another, envying one another. (Galatians 5:25-26)

• • •

We spend much of our conscious life crafting narratives in our heads of the things other people think about us. We spend our early developmental years supposing we are the subject of others' attention, judgment, and envy. We believe our identity is in what we do, how we look, who we are seen with, and what we own.

Then, mercifully, we grow up. We discover a deeper intuition, a wiser voice within ourselves that doesn't care about the drama of others' opinions. It knows that our value is not in our doing (though loving actions have deep value) but in our being. We learn to practice "presencing," deepening our awareness of God in us in every moment.

This awareness creates a certain humility. While we are accessing a deeper source of wisdom within, we are also forced to face our shadows. We see our selfishness, hypocrisy, manipulation, and insecurities, and realize we are not as good as we think we are or as holy as we wish we could be. Many of us can't handle that reality, so we embrace acts of denial—addiction, consumerism, mindless entertainment, and workaholism, to name a few—and our growth stops.

Unfortunately, facing our shadows is an essential step in our awakening. Saint John of the Cross called it "the Night of the Senses." In this space, you meet your raw, undefended, and indefensible self. This meeting destroys any illusion of your perfection and opens you to self-compassion. Here you learn of grace. Your sense of God's presence with you is more than a spiritual idea. It is a soulful, unconditionally loving experience. In God's accompaniment, you begin working on telling the truth of who you really are.

Dancing with the shadow teaches you to hold ambiguity and complexity. You come to terms with non-dual reality. You are both good and bad, light and shadow, whole and broken. When you finally accept that truth—and for most of us, it takes a long time—you experience a shift of being. The you that emerges understands the true power of kindness, gentleness, and compassion.

We live in a world calling for our awakening to the Way of Love. Let's hold the possibility that we have the power within us to save our planet. We begin by shifting our consciousness, facing our shadows, and ultimately transforming ourselves.

Reflection Questions

- What shadow behaviors get in the way of your happiness?
- When you hold the "both/and" truth of yourself—good and bad, whole and broken—what shifts within you?

In Prayer

Sacred One,

I give thanks for the Wise Ones,
the ones who don't take nonsense from anyone,
the ones who know what needs to be done,
for the sake of Sacred Love.

The Wise Ones understand that love is sometimes tough,
fear is never an excuse,
oppression demands confrontation,
for the sake of what we hold dear.

May I, through my clearing vision
of our broken open world,
begin to see that seed of calling you placed in me long ago,
I am One, too.

Amen.

Inclusion Wasn't Popular

Be strong and bold; have no fear or dread of them, because it is the Lord your God who goes with you; he will not fail you or forsake you. (Deuteronomy 31:6)

• • •

In 1942, Clarence Jordan and his wife decided to start Koinonia Farm in Americus, Georgia. Clarence grew up in Americus but went off to college at the University of Georgia and got a degree in agriculture. He went on to earn a PhD in Greek New Testament in Louisville but came back to Georgia to be a farmer, giving his farm a Greek name, Koinonia Farm.

Clarence decided to take the New Testament seriously and turned his farm into an interracial intentional Christian community. Black and white people lived together in harmony on this farm. Remember, this is 1942.

Clarence loved to tell a story about the time the KKK came to visit his farm. They came to the fence and asked to see him because his name was on the deed. He walked out and greeted them and said, "How can I help you?" They said, "We just wanted to come out and let you know that we don't let the sun set on people like you." He turned to them and gave them his broadest smile, and said, "I'm so pleased to meet you, gentlemen. I have been waiting my whole life to meet someone who can make the sun stand still." He said they chuckled a little bit, and then he changed the topic to talk about the peanut crop that year.

They left him alone for about ten years until the civil rights movement really got going, and they realized how subversive the farm actually was. The KKK started firebombing his roadside stands, and then they put an economic boycott on the pecans that the farm produced. You could not buy or sell pecans from Koinonia Farm in Americus, Georgia.

Clarence decided they had to change their marketing strategy and start a mail-order business. He decided their packaging would include the tagline, "Help us ship the nuts out of Georgia." Somehow Clarence, his family, and his farm have survived all these many years, knowing firsthand the cost and joy of discipleship.

Following a faith of radical inclusion is never popular. But in a world that always seems on the brink of unraveling, I am grateful for people like Clarence and his wife, who show us that commitment, courage, and creativity are the antidotes to all that divides us.

Reflection Questions

- What steps are you taking to learn about people and cultures that are different from your own?
- When have you stood up for others and what did it cost you? What difference did it make for you or them?

An Ethic of Love

Which of these three, do you think, was a neighbor to the man who fell into the hands of the robbers?" He said, "The one who showed him mercy." Jesus said to him, "Go and do likewise." (Luke 10: 36-37)

• • •

The Reverend Hill Carmichael once wrote about a conversation with a seminary professor that changed his understanding of the Parable of the Good Samaritan by saying:

> A few years ago, a seminary professor of mine decided to use the parable of the Good Samaritan to make a point about how fear influences the decisions we make. He turned to Luke 10 and began to read. I zoned out for a few minutes . . .
>
> After my professor finished reading, he looked up and said, "This is not a story about being nice. This is a story about the transformation of the world." All of the sudden, I was paying attention again. Then he went on to explain that Jesus is responding to a question by sharing that there are three types of people along the road between Jerusalem and Jericho.
>
> The first type are the robbers, whose ethic suggests that "what is yours is mine at whatever cost." The robbers will take whatever they need through violence, coercion and whatever means necessary. These are the people who will leave us physically, mentally and emotionally beaten and bruised along life's road with nothing left but our shallow breath.
>
> The second type of person to walk along the dangerous road between Jerusalem and Jericho is represented by the priest and the Levite, whose ethic suggests that "what is mine is mine, and I must protect it even if it means you get hurt in the process." They aren't bad people. Both the priest and the Levite are deeply respected in their communities. They very likely follow all the societal rules and norms. They sit on local boards. They pay their taxes on time and likely coach their son's or daughter's teams. They also show a great deal of love to those

within their immediate communities, but because of what crossing the road to help might cost them, they put their head down and go about their business. So, without even recognizing it, they do more harm than good. Their focus is inward toward their needs and the needs of those who are most like them. It's an ethic that leads the good and decent priest and Levite toward a life of valuing their reputations instead of relationships. And it often results in them choosing their own individual rights over the health and well-being of their neighbors.

Then there is the Samaritan, whose ethic is love. Along one of the most dangerous roads in all of history seems to live by a code that says, "what is mine is yours . . . if you have need of it."

My safety is yours . . . if you have need of it.
My security is yours . . . if you have need of it.
My resources are yours . . . if you have need of them.
My health is tied to your health.
My well-being is tied to your well-being.

Reverend Martin Luther King, Jr. preached on this text often and once said that the real difference between the priest and the Levite from the Samaritan is the question that each must have asked. The priest and the Levite likely asked, "If I stop to help this man, what will happen to me?" The Samaritan likely asked a very different question, "If I do not stop to help this man, what will happen to him?"

This story holds the tension of our faith. At the heart of good religion, we come to understand that we belong to one another. Our denial of that deep connection tears at our sacred fabric and endangers us all. That's the shock—it is not our diversity and connection that we need to fear; it is our illusion of difference and separation. That is the illusion that the Samaritan calls out.

Reflection Questions

- Today, as you interact with people, hold both questions in your mind: "If I care about this person, what will happen to me?" and "If I don't care about this person, what will happen to them?"

- How would you talk about your ethic of love? Write it out.

The Gift of Integrity

Let your eyes look directly forward, and your gaze be straight before you. Keep straight the path of your feet, and all your ways will be sure. Do not swerve to the right or to the left; turn your foot away from evil. (Proverbs 4:25-27)

• • •

I was sitting on the run-up pad in my plane going through my checklist. Free movement of my ailerons and rudder, check. All circuit breakers working, check. Altimeter set, check. Magnetos, check. Then I looked at my vacuum reading. It was showing zero pressure. I waited, hoping the engine just needed more time to warm up. It didn't move. I ran through the rest of my checklist. Everything checked out except the vacuum pump.

I sighed. I would not be flying that day.

I let the controllers in the tower know, and I taxied back to the ramp. Technically I could have flown according to the essential equipment list, but I risked my cabin filling with carbon monoxide if I had a serious problem. There was no way of knowing. I will fly anything with wings and an engine, but even I don't want to be thousands of feet in the air in a plane whose structural integrity is anything less than perfect.

Integrity is a hot topic today. Sometimes talked about in a moralistic frame, integrity better understood means that you are living in alignment with your values, in working order with how you are designed.

Many of us are waking up to a sense that the way we were working in the world before this pandemic was not aligned with how we are best designed. We are not designed to place profit over people. We are not designed to pollute our planet. We are not designed to discriminate against each other. We are not designed to harm each other.

Perhaps everything in our world seems to be falling apart because the world we have built lacks the integrity needed to take us forward. Perhaps we are being realigned, stripped down to the core of our design so that we can build a more inclusive society. We built a world that worked for some at the expense of others. That is not how God designed us. So, we taxi back to the hangar of our homes, schools and places of work to raise the hood and search for what has gone wrong. We look at our racism, our power dynamics, our laws, our assumptions, our pain, our ignorance, our hope, our desires . . .our deepest and truest values. We muster the courage to see what is broken and the humility to begin the fixes.

We know at the core of us—what is true in our design—is that we were built to fly in formation, together.

Reflection Questions

- What changes have you made in your life since the pandemic that you want to hold onto going forward?

- What changes do you want to make that more clearly express who you are and who you sense God calling you to be?

A More Perfect Union

Your kingdom come, your will be done, on earth as it is in heaven. (Matthew 6:10)

• • •

When I was a child going to school in Atlanta, Georgia, my teachers taught me that forming a "more perfect union" of freedom, equality and opportunity was the dream of democracy. "You are a citizen of this country," they said, "and your responsibility is to hold that dream—even fight for it—not for your individual benefit but for all of us."

As I grew older, this duty of citizenship became complicated. I realized that my white skin color opened doors of opportunity closed to people with darker skin. My economic class meant that I could go to college and work in an occupation of my choosing. My citizenship allowed me to pass through security lines without question while people from other parts of the world were stuck in systems of surveillance and suspicion.

Without question, I was FREER than many others. I had done nothing to earn or deserve such privilege. I was just lucky enough to be born white. I have benefited profoundly from that luck, and that isn't right.

Our nation was birthed with a flaw in our founding DNA—we were born in an unholy marriage of white nationalism and Christian exceptionalism. Our founding leaders held this truth to be self-evident: that all people, under God, must accept the superiority of whiteness. We continue that practice to this day.

Robert P. Jones, author of *White Too Long: The Legacy of White Supremacy in American Christianity*, puts it plainly: "On a broader level, white supremacy involves the way a society organizes itself, and what and whom it chooses to value . . . And that is white supremacy without all the bluster: a set of practices informed by the fundamental belief that white people are valued more than others."

We are locked in a battle as old as our nation. But for many of us, we are no longer willing to accept the superiority of whiteness. Many who have benefited from that privilege act from fear, expressed as hate. We must make sure that their actions fail.

In the 1950s, Reverend Dr. Martin Luther King Jr. popularized a vision of the "Beloved Community": a community in which everyone is cared for, absent of poverty, hunger, and hate. To achieve it, he said, we have to rebuild our systems currently steeped in racism and division.

The Christian life, he went on to note, is one built on brotherhood and sisterhood of ALL people. No one is better or worse in the eyes of God. No one matters more than another. We cannot be people of faith—any faith—and not live by that fundamental truth.

Educator and civil rights activist Robert Parris Moses warned us that the nation "can lurch backward as quickly as it can lurch forward." We must choose what kind of nation we will become. The scriptures tell us this: When we decide to live into the dream of freedom, equality, and opportunity for ALL of us, then we all thrive. That is the vision at the heart of the Lord's Prayer: "Your kingdom come, your will be done, on earth as in heaven."

Let's make it so.

Reflection Questions

- When did you become aware of your own race, that your skin color changed the way people treated you?

- How do you imagine God would form an ideal community? Who would have power? What values would we hold together?

In Prayer

Loving God,

Sometimes I can look at someone and see their pain. I can see their loneliness and feel their sadness. Sometimes I look in the mirror and see those things in me. Help me not turn away or ignore what I or others are really feeling. Give me patience to sit with my neighbors as they navigate their pain and welcome their accompaniment as I navigate my own. Through it all, help us all remember that we are not alone. You are with us always.

Amen

The Dakini Speaks

But where shall wisdom be found? And where is the place of understanding? Mortals do not know the way to it, and it is not found in the land of the living. (Job 28:12-13)

• • •

Tibetan Buddhism tells stories of the dakini, a wild, free sacred spirit who likes to pull the rug out from under us when we become too complacent. In her book *Wisdom Rising*, Lama Tsultrim Allione talks about the dakini this way:

> The dakini is a messenger of spaciousness and a force of truth, presiding over the funeral of self-deception. Wherever we cling, she cuts; whatever we think we can hide, even from ourselves, she reveals. The dakini traditionally appears during transitions: moments between worlds, between life and death, in visions between sleep and waking, in cemeteries and charnel grounds.

Something about the chaos of our world has drawn out of me a deep curiosity about the gifts granted in these transformational moments. What in us becomes whole by being broken? What gets revealed when we are stripped of certainty and our unquestioned assumptions?

In 2015, psychotherapist and spiritual teacher Jennifer Welwood wrote a poem that offers a beautiful invitation into this mystery.

> The Dakini Speaks
>
> My friends, let's grow up.
> Let's stop pretending we don't know the deal here.
> Or if we truly haven't noticed, let's wake up and notice.
> Look: Everything that can be lost, will be lost.
> It's simple—how could we have missed it for so long?
> Let's grieve our losses fully, like ripe human beings,
> But please, let's not be so shocked by them.
> Let's not act so betrayed,
> As though life had broken her secret promise to us.
> Impermanence is life's only promise to us,
> And she keeps it with ruthless impeccability.

To a child she seems cruel, but she is only wild,
And her compassion exquisitely precise:
Brilliantly penetrating, luminous with truth,
She strips away the unreal to show us the real.
This is the true ride—let's give ourselves to it!
Let's stop making deals for a safe passage:
There isn't one anyway, and the cost is too high.
We are not children anymore.
The true human adult gives everything for what cannot
be lost.

Let's dance the wild dance of no hope!

Does it feel as if our world is "coming of age"? The adolescent ways we treat one another and the planet don't work anymore. We don't get to live as if our actions don't have lasting consequences. They do. We are adults now. We have grown up over these past few years.

Being an adult means that we have the power to change. Like the wild dakini, we have power to show up as fierce and intense or playful and nurturing. We decide which world we wish to create, remembering the world which God has always dreamed for us. If I understand Jesus's ministry, this was his lasting message to us: we have the power, and responsibility, to create heaven on earth. We are not children anymore. We are in this together.

Reflection Questions

- Jennifer Welwood writes, "The true human adult gives everything for what cannot be lost." What does that mean to you?
- What does it mean in your own life to create heaven on earth?

How Do We Learn to Love?

"By this everyone will know that you are my disciples, if you love one another." (John 13:35)

• • •

In his book, *The Great Spiritual Migration*, Brian McLaren reflects on his transition from being a pastor of a congregation to being a member of one. He wondered if he would want to go to church at all and thought it would be easy to skip since no one was watching. What part of "church" would he miss? What could he live without? Here is what he discovered:

> . . . what I needed as a parishioner was very different from what had preoccupied me as a pastor. I wasn't looking for clever sermons or a certain style of music. I didn't need a church that was "cool" or "contemporary" or big or small. I certainly didn't need a church whose primary goal was to police the belief systems of its members.
>
> Instead, I wanted and needed a church that would help me live a life of love, with as little distraction as possible. I needed sustenance, encouragement, and help in loving God, loving myself, loving my wife, loving my kids and grandkids and extended family, loving my neighbors, especially people I might struggle to love, and loving the earth. I felt that without a community and regular gatherings to help me, I could too easily drift, too easily shift into autopilot, too easily stagnate and sour. Without intentional care and relevant practices, my soul could grow weary and cold, or go small and dark. I could lose my way. Easily.

Many of us are wondering how churches are changing and what they should look like in the future. Perhaps that is not the most important question. More pressing, it seems to me, is "How do I learn to live in deeply loving ways—so that I act, talk and walk like Jesus/Spirit—and what community can help me do that?"

Our religious traditions, at their best, are gifts that provide places and practices to draw us deeper into eternal wisdom. If they do not serve that purpose, we should abandon them in the heap of all else that we have learned to let go of this past year. Our calling is to follow the Way of God, the Way of Love, wherever it leads us.

Reflection Questions

- If you were intentionally living a life of love, what would be different about your life today?
- What do you need from a faith community? What do you wish to offer in return?

Make Your Religion Kindness

I give you a new commandment, that you love one another. Just as I have loved you, you also should love one another." (John 13:34)

• • •

Buddhism offers wonderful gifts to Christians. Where Christianity tends to obsess about doctrines and dogma, Buddhism stays focused on the "how." How do we live holy lives? How do we open ourselves to wisdom? How do we learn to love?

The Dalai Lama offers a beautiful teaching when he says, "My religion is kindness." Jesus taught something similar when he said, "I give you a new commandment, that you love one another. Just as I have loved you, you also should love one another." (John 13:34).

Love is the energetic current that orders and connects all that exists. As an expression of Sacred Love, kindness is a doorway to compassion, friendship, and belonging. If we all acted as if our religion was kindness, we would care deeply for one another and creation.

As I move more into contemplative practices, I am learning that practicing loving kindness grants an intuitive sense that everything is ultimately well. After a profound mystical experience, Julian of Norwich, an English anchoress of the Middle Ages, reflected on her insight into Love this way: "All shall be well, and all shall be well, and all manner of things shall be well."

That outlook seems insane in light of the challenges we face as a humanity. How can "all be well" when we kill black and brown lives? How can "all be well" as we pollute our planet? Our sense of "wellness" doesn't absolve us of our obligations to justice. We are not blind to injustice and suffering.

We are not "well" when we live from a dualistic mind. When we see the world as "us vs. them," "me over you," "good vs. bad," we deny the reality of our shared heritage—that we are all created in the image of God (Genesis 1:27). God is in us, and we are in God. Theologian Thomas

Aquinas taught us all of creation is in God and from God. It's all sacred.

When we start from an integrated (unified) consciousness, we see our interdependence as the ground of all truth. From that truth, we make the bold assertion that "all is well." Love is the source of all that exists. Because our being shapes our doing, justice that endures begins and ends with that truth.

Kindness becomes our religion because Love is our source. Let's practice the religion of kindness today.

Reflection Questions

- How does holding a sense of well-being open you to God?
- How have you learned to live a life of loving kindness? How could you deepen your practice?

Becoming Wise

And now faith, hope, and love abide, these three; and the greatest of these is love. (1 Corinthians 13:13)

• • •

In a recent conversation with the head of a university, I found myself reflecting on education in general by saying, "I don't need to read any more academic books unless they make me wise. I don't need to sit through any more lectures unless they teach me to become more fully present. I don't need to engage in any more practicums unless they help me become more kind. Can your program help people become wise, present and kind?"

It seems to me that should be the point of education. Why are we learning information to pass exams or defend dissertations? Education ultimately should be in service to making us more whole, awakened, intelligent souls. In the absence of that, it feels like we are all left to flounder on our own, starting at zero, with few mentors to guide us in the critically important task of becoming fully human.

The congregation is another space that should be dedicated to teaching us about wisdom, presence, and kindness. The church community, above all others, should be laser-focused on deepening our self-awareness and connecting our story to a larger story serving the common good. Without that larger story, the Great Tradition, we remain in patterns of violence, suffering, immaturity, and lethargy while we defend our small, delicate egos.

For our spiritual awakening to be authentic, we must begin that work from within. Who we are becomes the source for what we create. How we love ourselves fuels how we love others. How bravely we accept who we are determines how compassionately we embrace others.

Our modern education systems would have us believe the opposite—that what we acquire and achieve outside of ourselves opens the gate to deeper understanding within. This is the Big Lie of the me-first culture.

If we want to remake the world, we must first remake ourselves. To do that, we begin by learning what matters most: faith, hope and love.

But the greatest of these is love. (1 Corinthians 13:13)

Reflection Questions

- Who have been your best teachers in becoming wise, present, and kind?
- When you boil it all down, what has your faith in God taught you?

In Prayer

Let us desire nothing else
let us wish for nothing else
let nothing else please us and cause us delight
except our Creator and Redeemer and Savior,
the One True God, Who is the Fullness of Good,
all good, every good, the true and supreme Good;

Let nothing hinder us,
nothing separate us or nothing come between us.
May the power of your love O Lord, fiery and sweet as honey,
wean my heart from all that is under heaven,
so that I may die for love of your love
You who were so good as to die for love of my love.

Amen.

Here Begin the Terrors, Here Begin the Miracles

The Lord is my shepherd, I shall not want. He makes me lie down in green pastures; he leads me beside still waters; he restores my soul. He leads me in right paths for his name's sake. (Psalm 23:1-3)

• • •

A friend called with the news we would never wish on anyone. "My husband, John, has lung cancer," she said. "They say it's stage four. What are we going to do?"

My mind flashed to the first lines of the Grail Legends:
"Here is the Book of thy Decent,
Here begins the Book of the Holy Grail,
Here begin the terrors,
Here begin the miracles."
Here begin the terrors.

Of course, I had no answers. I thought of her two young children, too young to really understand the threat to their beautiful family. I thought of my friend, who had herself just recovered from breast cancer, now facing the harrowing journey of caring for her beloved husband. "I don't know what is going to happen," I said to her, "but you are not alone."

In the story of the Holy Grail, the young prince Parsifal, leaves the comfort of his royal life in search of the Grail, the ultimate prize of enlightenment. Professor Joseph Campbell talked about the Grail myth as "the search for the inexhaustible fountain, the search of one's life, even if that search should take us through the most terrible suffering. In fact, as the Grail teaches, it is the suffering itself that prepares us to receive the miracles."

Here begin the terrors, here begin the miracles.

My friend's husband was enrolled in a cancer treatment trial and went through many rounds of infusions, tests, and scans. At some appointments they received hopeful results only to have them dashed at the next one. It was a roller-coaster of terror and miracles, time gained and time lost.

John and I had the chance to talk about how he was handling the ride: "What I've learned is that life has always included death. I denied that for a long time. But now I understand that it's both life and death, sickness and health, weakness and strength, suffering and peace," he said. "It's both/and, not either/or. Once I accepted that, I stopped suffering. I was freed to fully live, fully love, to find true peace." He went on, "I don't want to die, but I am so glad that I learned how to live. I hope I can teach my kids that in my living and my dying." He passed away two months after that conversation.

Here begin the miracles.

At his funeral those of us who knew and loved John gathered in a sanctuary in Atlanta. We told stories of how he made us laugh, pranks he played, work he created, and how his beautiful life made ours so much better. We missed him to the core of our being. And then in the other room, a band started playing. The music got louder and then suddenly a Mardi Gras band was playing all around us, wildly costumed and blaring their horns in celebration.

We looked at each other confused. But then we remembered: It is both/and. Grief and celebration. Heartbreak and hope. "Good one, John," I thought. We need that reminder.

Reflection Questions

- What has grief taught you about love?
- What have the people that you have loved and lost taught you about living your own life?

Contemplative Prayer

Devote yourselves to prayer, keeping alert in it with thanksgiving. (Colossians 4:2)

• • •

Contemplative prayer can be traced to the desert fathers and mothers, early Benedictine monasticism, and early Catholic teachers like Saint Bonaventure and the Carmelites. But then, the teaching was largely lost. Almost no teachers taught contemplative prayer from the sixteenth century onward. If you learned the practice, you learned it on your own, following your own instincts and the guidance of the Spirit.

In the 1970s, Thomas Keating and a handful of other monks re-introduced Centering Prayer into Christianity. They knew it was an excellent portal drawing us into the silence essential to deepening our awareness of God within us.

Today, we need Centering Prayer more than ever before. It is a simple practice, but its power comes through repetition over time and patience with yourself.

As Episcopal priest and mystic Cynthia Bourgeault taught it to me, you begin by sitting comfortably with your eyes closed, relaxing into your breath. Become aware of God's presence within you. Choose a word or phrase that holds your desire to open yourself to God. It might be "Be still and know." It could also be something as simple as "Love" or "One" or "All."

Repeat that phrase slowly in your mind allowing everything else to fall away. Thoughts may arise. Simply acknowledge them and dismiss them, refocusing on your phrase or word.

Then, let the word or phrase drift away until you are held in simple stillness and peace. Stay there as long as you can or as long as you like.

Over time, this practice deepens your being and opens you to levels of knowing, present all along, but inaccessible to most. The only requirement to Centering Prayer is that you show up. The only way to fail is to quit. Its gifts are revealed in time and through practice.

"RESIST no thought; RETAIN no thought; REACT to no thought; RETURN to the sacred word," says Cynthia.

Perhaps try it for twenty minutes a day. What do you have to lose?

Reflection Questions

- How has prayer deepened your connection to God?
- If you would like a richer prayer life, what steps could you take today?

The Gift of Dark Nights

For I am convinced that neither death, nor life, nor angels, nor rulers, nor things present, nor things to come, nor powers, nor height, nor depth, nor anything else in all creation, will be able to separate us from the love of God in Christ Jesus our Lord. (Romans 8:38-39)

• • •

When Dr. Elizabeth Kübler Ross was writing her famous book *On Death and Dying*, part of her research involved interviewing dying patients in the hospital, trying to find out how they felt as they faced death. As she went from room to room in the hospital, she began to notice a remarkable pattern. Sometimes she would go into a dying person's room and the person would be calm, at peace, and tranquil. She also began to notice that often this was after the patient's room had been cleaned by a certain hospital orderly.

One day, Dr. Ross happened to run into this orderly in the hospital corridor, and she asked her, "What are you doing with my patients?"

The orderly thought she was being reprimanded by the doctor, and she said, "I'm not doing anything with your patients."

"No, no," responded Dr. Ross, "it's a good thing. After you go into their rooms, they seem at peace. What are you doing with my patients?"

"I just talk to them," the orderly said. "I've had two babies of my own die on my lap. But God never abandoned me. I tell them that. I tell them that they aren't alone, that God is with them, and that they don't have to be afraid."

Many of us have lost so much over the past few years. As a culture it feels as if we have descended into what Christian mystic, John of the Cross, called "the dark night of the soul." We are in a place of unknowing, between one world that we knew and one that we can't possibly predict.

In our waiting, our task is to learn to trust the journey. That is the magic of "dark nights." They last as long as they last, teaching us that being present, without expectation or obligation, opens the pathway to the deepest truth of all: No matter what, God is with us, and we are with God.

The Apostle Paul reminds us in Romans 8:38-39, "Neither death, nor life, nor angels, nor rulers, nor things present, nor things to come, nor powers, nor height, nor depth, nor anything else in all creation, will be able to separate us from the love of God in Christ Jesus our Lord."

Today, I give thanks for the orderly who knew that simple truth and could teach the rest of us something of faith, hope and love.

Reflection Questions

- What difference does it make to know that God is with you, that you are never abandoned or alone?
- What has prayer taught you about yourself? About God?

Hachiko and Lifelong Friendship

"Do not press me to leave you or to turn back from following you! Where you go, I will go; where you lodge, I will lodge; your people shall be my people, and your God my God." (Ruth 1:16)

• • •

Outside Shibuya Station in Tokyo stands a bronze statue of a dog named Hachiko. Hachiko was an Akita Inu dog born in 1923 and adopted by Hidesaburo Ueno, a professor of agriculture at the University of Tokyo. Each morning Ueno and Hachiko would walk together to the Shibuya train station where Ueno would tell the dog goodbye before getting on the train to work. Hachiko would then spend the day waiting for Ueno to come back. In the meantime, local shopkeepers and station workers would keep an eye on him and often give him treats while he held his vigil for Ueno.

This routine continued for two years until one day, Ueno never returned. While at work, he suffered a sudden brain hemorrhage and died. Hachiko moved in with a former gardener of the Ueno family. But throughout the rest of his ten-year life, he went to the Shibuya train station every morning and afternoon when the train was due to enter the station, to wait for Ueno.

Eventually, Hachiko passed away himself. His loyalty so moved the people who knew him that they put up the bronze statue as a reminder that friendship can last a lifetime.

This is Sacred Love. Love that doesn't forget, doesn't quit, doesn't fade. It just keeps showing up. It keeps faith in us. It holds hope that we will keep welcoming it as we walk home. This is the love God has for you.

Reflection Questions

- What have deep friendships taught you about God's love?
- What difference have friendships made in your life? In what ways do you want to be a better friend?

In Prayer

May God bless you, keep you, be gracious to you.
May God give you grace never to sell yourself—
or God—short.
Grace to risk something big for something good.
Grace to remember that the world is now too dangerous
for anything but truth,
And too small for anything but love.
So may God take your mind and think through it.
May God take your lips and speak through them.
May God take your hands and do good with them.
May God take your heart and set it on fire.

Amen.

It's All Grace

I praise you, for I am fearfully and wonderfully made. Wonderful are your works; that I know very well. (Psalm 139:14)

• • •

Celtic spiritual teacher and author John Philip Newell in his book *Sacred Earth, Sacred Soul* reminds us at just the right moment in human history of the gift of Celtic Christianity, a faith that honors the sacredness of the earth and of the human soul. For Celtic Christians, humanity and creation are interwoven in a beautiful tapestry of interdependence. "It's all One, everything connected to everything," the Celtic Christian might say.

In his opening chapter, Newell tells us the story of Pelagius, the Celtic monk who lived AD 360-430. Scholars remember him as a theological adversary to Augustine (which makes me like him immediately), though Newell goes to great lengths to clarify and redeem Pelagius' reputation.

Pelagius taught that it is not so much what you believe *about* Jesus that matters. The important thing is becoming *like* Jesus, becoming compassionate.

Pelagius says, "When Jesus commands us to love our neighbors, he does not only mean our human neighbors; he means all of the animals and birds, insects and plants, amongst whom we live." To do this, we must attend to five areas in our lives: the human soul, nature, spiritual practice, wisdom, and compassion. These represent a fully integrated human life, providing a "Rule of Life" that opens us to God.

"But," Pelagius says, "the starting place is to see that all of life is grace. This moment is grace. Nature is grace. The rising sun each day is grace. Life is a gift of God through grace. As we live with that awareness, we receive the grace of illumination. We awaken to the deep connection of all of creation, and we return to right relationship with ourselves and each other. When we falter, we learn about the grace of forgiveness or mercy. We fail, we betray, we fall short, and we learn to seek reconciliation and return to our true integrity."

I love this balance of attention and grace. "Pay attention to your sacred life," Pelagius says. "But when you lose yourself, there is grace. Then, try again."

In a time of human history when we live in such divisive and disconnected ways, I am grateful that Newell has reminded us of what our souls already know to be true: All good things come from God.

Our calling is to wake up to that Sacred Love that gave life to all that is. From there, we can reflect that love to others and all of the earth. Then we will be truly and fully alive.

Let's give it a try.

Reflection Questions

- What does grace mean to you?
- How would you like to become more like Jesus?

Scale Matters

Blessed are your eyes, for they see, and your ears, for they hear. (Matthew 13:16)

• • •

Every time I get in my airplane to fly, I am required to get a current weather report. In aviation lingo, it's called an ATIS (automatic terminal information service) report. I tune my communications to a designated frequency and listen to a recording that is updated about every twenty minutes by an air traffic controller. The report tells me about conditions at the airfield. I hear the latest wind direction and speeds, temperature, dewpoint, altimeter setting, and any service issues such as a taxiway closed or a lighting system out.

When I am coming in to land at an airfield, I repeat the same process. Ten miles out, I tune to the designated frequency, write down the critical information, and then calculate my approach to landing.

I have received hundreds of ATIS reports during my flying career. Never once has an ATIS report said "CAUTION: The surface of the earth is warming, and sea levels are rising." It has never once said "Notice to Airmen: Wildfires in the west are gaining in speed and intensity every year."

I receive weather reports almost every day, but they never tell me about the large-scale, major shifts in weather patterns that are changing our planet. They are not designed to. They are designed to tell me about the weather at my specific location at the surface. They are designed to speak to a certain reality at a certain altitude. But they leave me blind to the bigger weather picture threatening our collective survival.

Scale matters. This time of financial meltdown, climate breakdown, COVID lockdown, political letdown, and racial throwdown is revealing the global, systemic undoing of a world order that has finally run its course. Perhaps this moment was inevitable; we just didn't have access to a scale of vision to put all of the pieces together. Or perhaps we did and decided we didn't want to listen to that report.

You might remember in Matthew 13:16 when Jesus said, "Blessed are your eyes, for they see, and your ears, for they hear." He was praising the disciples for seeing beyond their comfort zones, beyond their normal perceptions, beyond their standard altitude.

So too must it be with us. The world is remaking itself, and the Spirit is moving in ways previously unseen. May we have the eyes to see, the ears to hear and courage to fly high. See you in the clouds.

Reflection Questions

- What scary, large-scale reality have you been avoiding seeing in your own life?
- How is God remaking the world? What can you, from your particular vantage point, see that the rest of us might miss?

Perennial Wisdom

In the beginning was the Word, and the Word was with God, and the Word was God. (John 1:1)

• • •

Perennial philosophy was first coined in the early sixteenth century by Italian humanist Agostino Steuco (1497-1548). It is a way of understanding wisdom from cultures around the world which basically boils down to four big ideas:

1. There is only one Reality (we have many names for it: God, Allah, Tao, Brahman, Great Spirit, Divine Feminine, Dharmakaya, Sophia, Obatala, Universe, . . .).

2. We are each a manifestation of this Reality, though most of us believe in a smaller, ego-based vision of ourselves.

3. This identification with a smaller vision of ourselves brings unnecessary suffering, anxiety, violence, and the illusion of separation.

4. Peace, compassion, and justice naturally replace these when we realize our truest manifestation of the Divine Reality.

The perennial wisdom tradition honors that in human cultures around the world and throughout time, we have created different religions, but we seem to be on the same journey. We are all exploring the questions of who we are, where we came from, and why we are here.

These are particularly important questions for this time, a time when we have developed technology powerful enough to both save the world and destroy it. Perennial wisdom tells us that we must embrace this evolutionary moment. Our evolutionary task is releasing this small vision of ourselves for the sake of a vision that is truer—we are sacred beings having a human experience.

For today, let's hold this possibility: We can create a more just and generous world because we are, in reality, just and generous beings. The change starts within each one of us and grows from there. We create the world, day by day, awakening by awakening, life by life. Upon this truth, the whole future of the world rests.

Reflection Questions

- What have other faith traditions taught you about living a good life? How does that reinforce or challenge your Christian faith?

- What difference do you want your life to make in your community? In the world?

The 4 H's

This is my commandment, that you love one another as I have loved you. No one has greater love than this, to lay down one's life for one's friends. (John 15:12-13)

• • •

Everything shut down in 2020 just when Kevin Stefanski was getting his footing as the Cleveland Browns' new head coach. He had been on the job for close to two months and had only recently closed on a house. His family was still in Minneapolis. His coaching staff had just been finalized, and the offices around him were starting to fill up. Players would return for workouts in a month, and preparations were underway to welcome them into a new culture, a new beginning, under his leadership.

But then, suddenly, everything had to be adjusted; the world was under COVID lockdown. Stefanski and all Browns employees were no longer permitted in the facility and would work remotely for an indefinite period starting March 13. Stefanski rejoined his family in Minneapolis and many of the team's other coaches returned to their previous residences. But the work continued.

Stefanski said he kept asking the question: "How do you come together when you're apart?"

In a meeting with Virginia Commonwealth University men's basketball coach Mike Rhoades, Stefanski learned about the "4 H's." To build a team spirit and help people get to know one another, Rhoades asked his players to talk about their:

— History
— Heroes
— Heartbreaks
— Hopes

It proved to be an incredibly powerful experience. Stefanski shamelessly stole the idea, asking his players to start their virtual season together sharing their 4 H's with the rest of the team. What followed was an epic comeback to their best season in decades.

Why do I tell you this story?

Because as my grandfather and UMC minister, Dr. Jim McCormick, often says, "Life is about relationships. The quality of our lives depends upon the quality of our relationships." This is how God designed us: to be beloved community, vulnerable in our sharing and generative in our acting. When we know one another, our sense of connection and belonging makes a kinder, safer, more equitable world possible.

So, my request of you is to invite people in your life—your family, your neighbors, your companies—to share their 4 H's. As author Pattie Digh says, "The shortest distance between two people is a story."

Reflection Questions

- What are your 4 H's?

- Whose story do you want or need to hear?

In Prayer

Spirit of God,

Open our eyes to see you,
Open our ears to hear you,
Open our hands to touch you,
Open our hearts to hold you,
Open our souls to welcome you.

In our opening,
may we know Peace,
may we know Joy,
may we know Love.

Amen and amen.

The Message of the Hawk

The Lord bless you and keep you; the Lord make his face to shine upon you, and be gracious to you; the Lord lift up his countenance upon you, and give you peace. (Numbers 6:24-26)

• • •

Many mornings I begin my day enjoying my coffee while sitting outside on our dock by the lake. Over time I have become familiar with the wondrous life of this place. Colorful songbirds serenade me from the trees. Celebrating the addition of six new babies, the geese come swimming along in a line to say good morning. Last year someone abandoned two white baby ducks in the lake. I have watched them grow up, befriending the geese and herons that hang out in our spot on the water.

Some mornings as we are all sitting in communion, our peace will be startled by the shrill cry of a soaring hawk. We all look up at her, seeing if we can spot what is creating all the commotion.

In their book on indigenous traditions called *Medicine Cards: The Discovery of Power Through the Ways of Animals*, Jamie Sams and David Carson teach about the Hawk:

> The Ancients recognized this magnificent bird of prey as a messenger bringing tidings to their Earth Walk. . . . A Hawk may be bringing you the message that you should circle over your life and examine it from a higher perspective. From this vantage point, you may be able to discern the hazards which bar you from freedom of flight. Remember: The Hawk has a keen eye and a bold heart, for the Hawk flies close to the light of the Sun.

Theologian and mystic Meister Eckhart says, "Anyone who truly knows creatures may be excused from listening to sermons, for every creature is full of God, and is a book."

When the hawk flies overhead in the mornings, I look up with curiosity and awe. She draws my attention to a higher place of seeing. After reading Sams and Carson's description, I give thanks for that "call and response," for it now also draws me to a place of higher being. She keeps me awake, paying attention to life when it would be easy to zone out in distraction.

I hope a hawk shows up for you today, even if it doesn't have feathers and beaks and claws. Hawks are all around us if we have the eyes to see and ears to hear. We can spot them because they have one distinct call: "See your life with keen eyes and a bold heart. You, too, precious one, are full of God and meant to fly."

Reflection Questions

- What might you see or sense if you, like the hawk, circled over your life from a higher perspective?
- What lessons have animals taught you about life and living?

Why Do We Cause Harm?

"You shall love the Lord your God with all your heart, and with all your soul, and with all your mind.' This is the greatest and first commandment. And a second is like it: 'You shall love your neighbor as yourself.' On these two commandments hang all the law and the prophets." (Matthew 22:37-40)

• • •

Living in the United States means we live in a nation with significant gun violence. But living almost anywhere in the world at this point means we live in contexts where violence can tear through communities.

Why do we keep killing each other?

Why are we choosing to live in an ultraviolent state,
ruled by domination and aggression?

Why are we risking our children's lives? Black lives? Brown lives?

Why are we shaping a culture that demands we become numb
so that we aren't crushed with grief?

Why aren't we talking about toxic masculinity?

Why aren't we treating white supremacy as terrorism?

Why?

Journalist Jonathan Thompson recently observed this pattern of trauma by saying, "Each incident tears at the fabric of society and the collective psyche. The epidemic of mass shootings in America is perhaps the most effective act of terrorism ever inflicted, in that it injects us all with a little nodule of terror that re-emerges every time we send our kid to school or our spouse to the grocery store, vaguely wondering whether they'll come back."

What a heartbreaking reality we have created. Because of our manufactured fear of one another and our greed for power over others and our planet, we have shaped a culture steeped in abuse, trauma, and grief. Surely, we want more for ourselves. Surely, we want more for our children?

Philosopher and environmental activist Joanna Macy once told a story about working with a community devastated by the Chernobyl catastrophe. The people living in the impacted areas struggled to talk about the trauma. It felt too risky. Here is what she said to them:

> I have no wisdom with which to meet your grief. But I can share this with you: After the war that almost destroyed their country, the German people determined they would do anything to spare their children the suffering they had known. They worked hard to provide them a safe, rich life. They created an economic miracle. They gave their children everything—except for one thing. They did not give them their broken hearts. And their children have never forgiven them.

This is my great fear. Our children will never forgive us. They should not, for we are creating a world where their lives are in endless peril.

To stop this devastating cycle, we must share our heartbreak at allowing fear to drive us to division, greed to drive us to oppression, and ego to drive us to violence. In not facing what we have created, we deny us all the chance to correct what has gone awry between us.

When asked what was the greatest commandment, the commandment that spoke to the world as God dreamed it to be, Jesus gave a clear response: "'You shall love the Lord your God with all your heart, and with all your soul, and with all your mind.' This is the greatest and first commandment. And a second is like it: 'You shall love your neighbor as yourself.' On these two commandments hang all the law and the prophets."

Love God. Love your neighbor. Love yourself. Read that once more.

Reflection Questions

- What does it mean in your life to love your neighbor as yourself?
- If you shared your heartbreak with people you are close to, what might happen?

Who Is Really Insane?

Religion that is pure and undefiled before God, the Father, is this: to care for orphans and widows in their distress, and to keep oneself unstained by the world. (James 1:27)

• • •

The King of Hearts was filmed in 1966 and set in France in the midst of WWII. The Nazis were invading a small town, and a young Scottish soldier was sent to evacuate the town and secure the bomb store. Before he could accomplish his task, the Nazis came marching through. Suddenly the Scottish soldier needed to hide in order to evade capture. In a moment of desperation, he ran through gates that led to a large building with lots of windows. Racing up the stairs he was met by a group of people dressed in hospital gowns, some playing cards, others dancing, others holding baby dolls and telling stories.

It hit him, then. This was an insane asylum.

He had no choice. With the Nazi soldiers close on his tail, he adorned one of the robes and tried to fit into the group. The soldiers came and didn't spot him. When they left (leaving the gate to the asylum open for the residents to leave), the residents of the asylum looked at the soldier and asked who he was. Speechless, he said nothing. But then someone shouted out, "He is the king! The king has returned."

With that declaration, the residents broke into a joyful dance. They flooded out of the gates into the streets. They found new clothes to wear in the abandoned shops and absconded with carts to use for a parade. They dressed in what felt right to them—one a Catholic cardinal, one a circus master, one a ballerina, one a prostitute. They held a coronation and showered the new king with kind words and generous gifts.

The Nazi soldiers were marching through the streets at that point, throwing people to the ground, terrifying them and threatening their lives. But here were these people labeled "insane" by the world, celebrating freely, caring for each other, making one another laugh, honoring their truest expressions, and being gentle with each other's needs. The Scottish soldier looked out at the street and then back at his new friends and, for the first time, found himself wondering who was truly insane.

It is a silly movie, full of slapstick humor. And then it smacks you between the eyes with the unvarnished truth. Maybe we are the ones who are insane?

If you ever wonder whether the values of our world seem backward, you're in good company. I suspect many of us have a growing sense that the values we have inherited in modern culture are not so valuable; that the morality we see in our systems, leaders, and media is not so moral. It's tempting to want to say "I'm out. I don't want to be associated with any of this anymore."

If that is where you are, I think we have every reason to be hopeful. Why? Because when we identify the way of life we don't want, we can finally choose something different. If you tune your ears to the prophets of all ages and traditions, they tell us time and time again that the values of community, love, generosity, and compassion reveal the truest expression of the human soul. These are the sacred values that shape a rightly ordered world that honors all of us.

Let's start creating that world with wild abandon, eccentric outfits, and relentless hope. It might be the sanest thing we could ever do.

Reflection Questions

- What values define and guide your life?

- How does the world feel insane to you? How does your understanding of God's love, kindness and care for the vulnerable show you what needs to be fixed?

In Prayer

Sacred One,

In the face of great need,
When the work feels huge
and I feel small,
may I learn of the power of
the mustard seed.

May I trust that my showing up,
Taking root,
Growing branches,
be enough to do
small great things that heal the world.

Amen.

Doing Meaningful Work

Let the favor of the Lord our God be upon us, and prosper for us the work of our hands—O prosper the work of our hands! (Psalm 90:17)

• • •

According to the US Labor Department's Job Openings and Labor Turnover Summary, thirty-eight million people in the United States quit their jobs in 2021. That represents more resignations than at any previous time in their twenty years of recording. Journalists have started referring to this trend as "The Great Resignation." Those paying attention saw this trend coming. They point out that people delayed normal job transitions because of the uncertainty created during the pandemic. Others discovered they want to do different kinds of work or work in different ways. These all are true to a point.

I believe something more significant is shifting.

For some of us, these days of deep disruption have become the birthing space for a new human dream—a dream of a world where we can earn a living while also living a balanced, awakened life. In her book, *Working Ourselves to Death*, Diane Fassel observes, "Because work addiction keeps us busy, we stay estranged from our essential selves. An aspect of that estrangement is that we cease asking ourselves if we are doing our right work. Are we actually doing our true work, performing tasks or pursuing vocations that are good for us, for our families, and the universe?"

This is the question that began haunting many of us at the beginning of the pandemic and has now fundamentally changed our imagination when it comes to work. Are we doing our right work? Are we pursuing vocations that are good for us, for our families, and for the planet?

In his book, *The Reinvention of Work,* priest and theologian Matthew Fox says, "Work comes from inside out; work is the expression of our soul, our inner being. It is unique to the individual; it is creative. Work is an expression of the spirit at work in the world through us. Work is that which puts us in touch with others, not so much at the level of personal interaction, but at the level of service in the community."

Fox is saying that right work, work that taps into the truest parts of our being, doesn't begin with doing but rather begins with being.

We need a new story about the function of work in our global culture. The industrial story—one of endless production and competitive power—is killing us and our planet. It has now reached the point of desperation, as we watch the mass extinction of thousands of species, the warming of our planet, the toxic pollution of our food and water sources, and the extreme strengthening of weather patterns across the globe.

The new story of work, which you and I are creating this very moment, has a few critical contours. The new story of work:

— Celebrates the diversity of cultures around the globe and generates systems of genuine inclusion.

— Seeks trusting relationships over transactional exchanges.

— Rewards inner contemplation as much as outer action.

— Understands work as a unique expression of each person's creativity, used for the benefit of the common good.

— Protects the planet as our first responsibility and highest privilege.

— Honors ancestral wisdom as well as scientific knowledge.

— Recognizes creative chaos/freedom is necessary for innovation. (Control is not an antidote.)

— Embraces "power with," never "power over."

— Sees our interdependence with each other and all living beings and works for the health, wholeness, and well-being of all.

— Treats work as a vocation, creating jobs that create a more just and sustainable world for all.

In the end, our "work" is part of the ongoing work of the universe. We are not the only workers busy creating and generating. Stars and galaxies, trees and rivers, flowers and birds, goats and bees—all of them have work to do. All of them spend their days creatively making the world a bit more beautiful. Interesting that they have no concept of unemployment. They never resign. Why? Because they have built a way of life that sees the point of it all—trusting that there will be enough, they do their work of creating beauty for the benefit of all of us, with wonder and awe. So, too, should we.

Reflection Questions

- If work is an expression of the spirit at work in the world through us, how does that shift your understanding of how you spend your days?
- What work are you being called to offer into the world?

Staying True to Ourselves

> *Do not be conformed to this world, but be transformed by the renewing of your minds, so that you may discern what is the will of God—what is good and acceptable and perfect. (Romans 12:2)*

• • •

In Cynthia Bourgeault's book, *Centering Prayer and Inner Awakening,* she talks about the challenge of staying true to ourselves. It's essential, she says, because our mind likes to get hooked on imagined dramas and react from insecurity. This reactivity distracts us from remaining aware of our true selves, our deeper awareness. In a model she calls "the False Self in Action," she says that our egos react to three emotional "programs." We are almost always acting out of our need for:

— Power/control

— Esteem/affection

— Security/survival

It's not necessarily harmful to act from these places. The harm comes when we do so unconsciously. It is then that we operate from hidden agendas. We start striving for power over others but denying that we are after control. Or we manipulate people for praise and affection from a sense of narcissistic arrogance rather than genuine relationship. When we become conscious of these patterns in ourselves, we can then make a decision. We can decide if behaving this way is authentic or if we are playing games. When we have the power to choose, we make better choices.

When I read Cynthia's words, I could see this pattern in my own life. Most of us never intend harm. But most of us aren't fully conscious of our motivations either. The invitation in Cynthia's work is to become conscious, to take responsibility for our actions so that our emotional health and our actions with and for others are the truest and highest expressions of our souls.

I accept that challenge and want to invite you to join in as well. Let's pay attention to our emotional "programs" and how we are using them with each other. When we notice that we are being triggered, Cynthia offers a simple litany, written by her friend, Mary Mrozowski, to help us find our way back:

> I let go of my desire for security and survival.
> I let go of my desire for esteem and affection.
> I let go of my desire for power and control.
> I let go of my desire to change the situation.

In the letting go, we discover that we must hold on to our integrity. "Wisdom isn't about knowing more," Cynthia says. "It's about knowing with more of you."

Reflection Questions

- How have you observed your "False Self in Action?" In what ways do you follow the programs of power/control; esteem/affection; or security/survival?

- What would it take to let go?

Living in Interesting Times

Then the Lord answered me and said: Write the vision; make it plain on tablets, so that a runner may read it. (Habakkuk 2:2)

• • •

In 1889, Charles H. Duell was the Commissioner of the US patent office. Reflecting on his office issuing the 500th patent, he predicted that the patent office would soon shrink in size, and eventually close. According to his assessment, "everything that can be invented has been invented." Today, that office has issued well over ten million patents.

Being able to sense the future is a valuable leadership skill in the world today. We read Duell's words and think "Wow, he was really out of touch." But I also wonder what assumptions you and I hold about our futures that could be as far off base and limited in scale. How are we holding ourselves back because we have a narrow view of a possible world?

Interestingly, it took 155 years, from 1836 to 1991, for the United States to issue its first five million patents. It took just twenty-seven years to issue the next five million.

The ancient curse "may you live in interesting times" has come true for us. This is it—the most interesting time in human history. As contemporary philosopher Jean Houston often reflects, "You and I are living 10 to 100 times the life experiences of our ancestors just one or two generations before."

Every day our lives reflect a quantum leap in complexity, innovation, and experience. So, what shall we do with this moment of opportunity? How shall we prepare?

Houston goes on to observe the essential work of expanding our vision—our consciousness—of ourselves and our world. "Extremely limited consciousness," she says, "gives us governments that are too large for the small problems of life and too small in spirit for the large problems. Extremely limited consciousness cannot deal with ethnic and tribal violence and the rage of the dispossessed, the addiction to consumption and soul-killing substances, the very survival of the planet. Instead, extremely limited consciousness offers us a patchwork quilt of solutions that create ten new problems for each quick fix."

In the face of great change, we need great vision. But don't be deceived into thinking we are waiting on some grand savior to make everything right. We are waiting on YOU. We are waiting on US. We are the dreamers, leaders, future makers and inventors. We need only claim in ourselves what has always been true.

Reflection Questions

- What in your life gives you hope for the future?
- What is your vision for a more just and generous world?

A Vision of Love

There is no fear in love, but perfect love casts out fear; for fear has to do with punishment, and whoever fears has not reached perfection in love. (1 John 4:18)

• • •

Author Mirabai Starr tells a story about Saint Francis of Assisi and his brilliant, subversive, loving approach to reforming the church leaders of his day. His teachings were unique among traditional Catholic priests and scholars. Powerful church leaders began to feel threatened by his vision of the world and the positive ways people were responding. They began questioning his authority and his approach. But instead of being defensive or pushing back against them, he confronted them gently. He didn't tell them that they were wrong; instead, he disarmed them with kindness and helped them see that there was a better way through love.

Starr reminds us that we need both. We need the activists and agitators who can speak truth to power with conviction and force. But we also need the lovers, healers, and teachers who speak their truth in ways that disarm the challengers and invite deep transformation. I suspect most of us find our natural home in one of these labels, but we hold all of these magical energies within us.

I am struck by the care Saint Francis took in teaching his vision of love. I suspect it was so powerful, even to this day, because he lived it as well.

This is my hope for us. I hope that we are all reading these wonderful texts and learning from incredible teachers. But even more, I hope we are living a life so powerfully rooted in love that our essence is the true teacher. Like Saint Francis, may we learn that it is not as much what we do, but more who we are, that invites others to put down their defenses and take up the Way of Love.

Reflection Questions

- What does living "the Way of Love" mean to you?
- When have you faced opposition and responded with love rather than defensiveness? What happened?

The Gift of Being Seen

He answered, "I was sent only to the lost sheep of the house of Israel." But she came and knelt before him, saying, "Lord, help me." (Matthew 15:24-25)

• • •

I was sitting with a friend of mine on a park bench in Piedmont Park in Atlanta. She was telling me about a devastating experience that she had as a child. She was abused and tortured by family members until she finally escaped her home at fifteen years old. The pain of her experience was palpable. My heart broke for her, even as I marveled at the extraordinary woman that she had become.

In response, I did what seemed natural. Feeling righteous indignation for her suffering, I started trying to fix it. I said, "Were they persecuted? Can we do that now? There have to be consequences!" I began spinning with idea after idea trying to make her pain not so bad, the injustice not so great.

Kindly, she reached over and took my hand. She said, "Cameron, your kindness means the world to me. I don't need you to fix me. I need you to hear me. I just need to be seen."

I think about that moment a great deal in these broken, painful days. We do have much we need to fix. But we also have many among us who simply need to be seen. We are doubled over with grief. We are buried by demands of work, family, and homeschooling. We are unemployed and terrified of losing everything. We are isolated and alone.

Being seen and heard in the midst of our pain is deeply healing. Listening creates relationship. We all have a story and want to share our story in order to be connected. That connection creates the healing we all so desperately need.

The Gospels tell a story about a Canaanite woman whose daughter was ill. She went to Jesus and begged him to help her. Jesus ignored her and the disciples complained about her. "Send her away!" they said. But she kept begging for help. "SEE ME, " she was saying. "Hear my story."

Jesus looked at her then and said something shocking: "It's not right to take bread out of children's mouths and throw it to dogs." She came back: "But beggar dogs do get scraps from the master's table." It was then, in the face of her vulnerability and her courage, that Jesus finally saw, finally heard her humanity connecting to his own. The woman's daughter healed.

It's a strange story but one that has taught me much over the years. Seeing and hearing each other is hard, even for the most enlightened among us. But when it finally happens, when we allow for genuine connection, we become a bit more whole.

May it be true for us in the beautiful and heartbreaking days.

Reflection Questions

- Reflecting on the story of the Canaanite woman, who in your life is asking to be seen and heard?
- Putting yourself in the shoes of the Canaanite woman, what do you wish others would see in you and hear in your story?

In Prayer

Blessed are you
who are filled with the fire of compassion,
the courage of vision,
the peace of hope
and the endurance of love,
for you will awaken to the Sacred One
who is awakening within you.

Amen.

Where Stories Come From

The wolf shall live with the lamb, the leopard shall lie down with the kid, the calf and the lion and the fatling together, and a little child shall lead them. (Isaiah 11:6)

• • •

In her book *The Faithful Gardener*, Dr. Clarissa Pinkola Estés talks about her childhood family ritual. She writes,

> In my family, the old ones practiced a tradition called "Make-Story," this being a time—often over a meal rich in aromas of fresh onions, warm bread, and spicy rice sausage—when the elders encourage the young to weave tails, poems, and other pieces. The old ones laughed with one another as they ate. To us they said, "We are going to test you to see if you were gaining any knowledge worth having. Come, come now, give us a story from scratch. Let us see you flex your story muscles."

What a wonderful and generous invitation to give to children. In essence, they were asking them to partner with them in imagining a new, shared world.

We need a new story, a new shared narrative of the kind of world we want to create together. The old story that we've told for so many years—the one of endless consumerism, oppressive power, class systems, and white supremacy—has run its course, and we should no longer tell it. It's a story that now hurts us more than helps us, tears us apart more than brings us together, and threatens our planet in apocalyptic ways.

We need a new story. We need a new future.

Some among us are beginning to talk about different ways of being and different futures possible for us all. They're talking about interdependence and eco-civilizations. They are speaking to dynamics of "power with" instead of "power over." They dream of a life that is defined by balance, collaboration, and work that aligns with our passions. These are the stories I love to hear.

Professor Otto Scharmer, in his book *Theory U: Leading from the Future as It Emerges*, says, "The real battle in the world today is not among civilizations or cultures but among the different evolutionary futures that are possible for us and our species right now. What is at stake is nothing less than the choice of who we are, who we want to be, and where we want to take the world we live in. The real question, then, is 'What are we here for?'"

We need a new story. We need a new future. What is the story we want to tell?

Reflection Questions

- What is the story within us that wants to be told?
- What is the story obvious to you, but perhaps not to others, that could offer a new vision for a new and better world?

The Shambhala Warrior

But the wisdom from above is first pure, then peaceable, gentle, willing to yield, full of mercy and good fruits, without a trace of partiality or hypocrisy. (James 3:17)

• • •

One of my favorite stories is a Tibetan Buddhist fable called the "Shambhala Warrior." Over twelve centuries old, the story of the Shambhala Warrior teaches us that the world will be healed not through violence or aggression but through gentleness, courage, and self-knowledge. We discover the basic goodness of human life and radiate that goodness out into the world for the peace and sanity of others.

Author and activist, Joanna Macy, shares this version, from her conversation with Dru-gu Choegyal Rinpoche. He says,

> "There comes a time when all life on Earth is in danger. Barbarian powers have arisen. Although they waste their wealth in preparations to annihilate each other, they have much in common: weapons of unfathomable devastation and technologies that lay waste the world. It is now, when the future of all beings hangs by the frailest of threads, that the kingdom of Shambhala emerges.
>
> -"You cannot go there, for it is not a place. It exists in the hearts and minds of the Shambhala warriors. But you cannot recognize a Shambhala warrior by sight, for there is no uniform or insignia, there are no banners. And there are no barricades from which to threaten the enemy, for the Shambhala warriors have no land of their own. Always they move on the terrain of the barbarians themselves.
>
> "Now comes the time when great courage is required of the Shambhala warriors, moral and physical courage. For they must go into the very heart of the barbarian power and dismantle the weapons. To remove these weapons, in every sense of the word, they must go into the corridors of power where the decisions are made.

> "The Shambhala warriors know they can do this because the weapons are manomaya, mind-made. This is very important to remember. These weapons are made by the human mind. So they can be unmade by the human mind! The Shambhala warriors know that the dangers that threaten life on Earth do not come from evil deities or extraterrestrial powers. They arise from our own choices and relationships. So, now, the Shambhala warriors must go into training."
>
> "How do they train?" I asked.
>
> "They train in the use of two weapons. The weapons are compassion and insight. Both are necessary. We need this first one," he said, lifting his right hand, "because it provides us the fuel, it moves us out to act on behalf of other beings. But by itself it can burn us out. So we need the second as well, which is insight into the dependent co-arising of all things. It lets us see that the battle is not between good people and bad people, for the line between good and evil runs through every human heart. We realize that we are interconnected, as in a web, and that each act with pure motivation affects the entire web, bringing consequences we cannot measure or even see.
>
> "But insight alone," he said, "can seem too cool to keep us going. So we need as well the heat of compassion, our openness to the world's pain. Both weapons or tools are necessary to the Shambhala warrior."

Good religion, coming from the rich wisdom traditions of all our world religions, point to this essential truth: Everything is interdependent, and love/compassion are the highest work of the soul. Jesus taught us this. The prophets taught us this. The mystics taught us this. Muhammad taught us this. And today, the Buddhist tradition teaches us this once again.

Reflection Questions

- What lessons for your own life can you take from the story of the Shambhala warriors?
- What conflict in your life could be lessened if you approached it mindfully with insight and compassion?

The Price of Failed Leadership

Do to others as you would have them do to you. (Luke 6:31)

• • •

"We wouldn't be shooting it down. We'd be ramming the aircraft . . . I would essentially be a kamikaze pilot," Maj. Heather Penney recalled about her flight on September 11, 2001.

On that day, Penney, then a lieutenant of the District of Columbia Air National Guard, had her orders. She had to intercept and stop United Airlines Flight 93 from making it to Washington, DC. But neither she nor her commander, who was in another fighter, ready to go, had any weapons to fire at the hijacked jet. The jets only had dummy bullets, still loaded after a training mission. So, the plan was, if necessary, to fly straight into the passenger jet. If she did that, she would die.

It turned out that the heroes that day were the brave passengers on Flight 93 who took the plane down themselves. But Maj. Penney was prepared to fulfill her oath to protect and defend the Constitution with her life if necessary.

I was thinking about Maj. Penney amid the current divisive political climate we see across the world. Leadership requires acts of profound courage in the face of fear, wisdom in the face of uncertainty, integrity in the face of compromise, and determination in the face of opposition.

Leadership begins within each of us. If we act with integrity privately, we lead with integrity publicly. If we are trustworthy and honest with ourselves, we are trustworthy and honest with others. Our actions are a byproduct of our personal authenticity. This principle is at the heart of our most powerful sacred stories in scripture. Over and over, our sacred texts tell us, "Do to others as you would have them do to you." (Luke 6:31). Keep straight the path of your feet, and all your ways will be sure. Do not swerve to the right or to the left; turn your foot away from evil. (Proverbs 4:26-27)."

Who we are shapes what we do, for good and ill. We stand at an evolutionary moment where who we become can shape a better world for our children and grandchildren in future generations. I pray we become more inclusive, kinder and more compassionate. I pray we learn to welcome the stranger, care for the poor, and strive for equality for all. I pray we become more Christlike so that when we look at one another, we see the face of God.

Reflection Questions

- How would you define leadership for yourself?
- What responsibilities come with leadership as Jesus modeled it?

A Just Economy for A Better World

> *How does God's love abide in anyone who has the world's goods and sees a brother or sister in need and yet refuses help? Little children, let us love, not in word or speech, but in truth and action." (1 John 3:17-18)*

• • •

One of the encouraging byproducts of this time of global lockdown has been the increased curiosity about a global economy that honors people, profit and the planet. More and more books are being published about eco-civilizations built on an economic philosophy that is just and generous. Entire schools of thought like Modern Monetary Theory offer us new visions of how we can do well while also doing good. I find these ideas hopeful and compelling.

What is less clear is how we move from the capitalist system we have to a system that honors what most of us value. How do we create a way of relating to one another that respects our planet, distributes power equitably, and honors all of God's creation?

I remember hearing a lecture by Dr. Walter Brueggemann some years ago when he described the biblical economic story something like this:

- We begin in the predatory slave economy of Pharaoh.
- Biblical faith is about emancipation from a predatory economy to an alternative economy.
- Bread from heaven signifies an unexpected abundance.
- The Ten Commandments at Mt. Sinai are a way to administer abundance.

From there, scripture becomes a wrestling match of competing views of how power should flow and ultimately who would be in control. It turns out the Ten Commandments were not popular with those invested in oppression.

Purity laws of the Old Testament became the way we decided. When we determine an entire class of people to be less pure—women, gays, people of color, immigrants—and we ritually demean them, it becomes a natural next step to economically exploit them. It seems we are still entangled in that destructive way of thinking.

But it is all falling apart. Finally, today, we are seeing signs that more and more of us want a new way, a different way of honoring our value and meeting our needs. Let's start by changing the risk/reward equation. Let's make the actions and products that hurt people and the planet LESS profitable and LESS desirable:

— Let's work to make giving someone healthcare more profitable than denying them.
— Let's work to make maintaining peace more profitable than going to war.
— Let's work to make protecting women's rights and freedom more profitable than selling them to human traffickers.
— Let's work to make investing in under-resourced communities more profitable than jailing black and brown people.

Do you see where I am going with this?

Let's work toward an economy that shapes a better world for all of us. Jesus talked about money more than any other topic during his ministry among us. There's a reason for that. We can't love God and oppress each other.

1 John 3:17-18 says it best: "How does God's love abide in anyone who has the world's goods and sees a brother or sister in need and yet refuses help? Little children, let us love, not in word or speech, but in truth and action."

Reflection Questions

- In what ways are you mindful of how you use your money to create a more just and generous world?

- What value systems can you influence (at work, in your family, in your community) to take care of the poor and disadvantaged?

In Prayer

May the wisdom of our elders be
written upon our hearts,
May the presence of the Saints
be woven into our beings,
May the peace of Christ be
with us always,
for all the days of our lives.

Amen

A Reframe

"You have heard that it was said, 'You shall love your neighbor and hate your enemy.' But I say to you, Love your enemies and pray for those who persecute you." (Matthew 5:43-44)

• • •

Recently I've been learning from a brilliant woman named Loes Damhof. She is a professor at Hanze University in the Netherlands specializing in a field of study called futures literacy. She guides people to think about the space between their probable future and their preferred future, inviting them to consider possibilities they would not have entertained before. It is a way of opening imagination and then acting to create a more beautiful life.

On a recent call, she said something that caught my attention about the importance of this work. She said, "Some people are colonizing our futures. They are setting the parameters today for the probable world we live in tomorrow. We don't have to let them. We can imagine a different preferred future and act to create it. The future is not determined." (Yes!)

The starting place, she explains, is to question the assumptions that we hold in the present. The opening of our imagination, or what she calls the reframe, starts with the phrase, "What if?"

Here are reframes to play with:

> What if you can't fail at what you are scared to try? What becomes possible?
>
> What if you don't work more than eight hours a day? What entices you?
>
> What if you put your phone in another room when you go to bed? What shifts in you?
>
> What if you focus more on being instead of doing? What becomes clearer to you?

What if you actually believed that God/Source loves you? What opens within you?

In giving voice to a preferred future in the face of a probable one, it occurs to me that Loes is practicing the art of prophetic proclamation. The prophets of our past and present all speak with a pattern of "You have heard it said (probable future) . . ., but I say (preferred future) . . ."

Matthew 5:43-44 models this through Jesus's words: "You have heard that it was said, 'You shall love your neighbor and hate your enemy.' But I say to you, Love your enemies and pray for those who persecute you."

In other words, "You have been told to believe this about the world, but I see a new possibility for how we can live together in peace." Whether it is called prophetic imagination or futures literacy, dreaming and working for a better future is the human journey at its best.

Our lives go through reframes. The question always before us is "What is our preferred future?" I can't help but wonder . . .what if we created a more just and generous world for all of us?

Reflection Questions

- What is your probable future if you continue on course in the direction you are currently heading?
- What is your desirable future? Is there a difference?

Breakdown and Breakthrough

Bear one another's burdens, and in this way you will fulfill the law of Christ. (Galatians 6:2)

• • •

Recently a friend sent me a text that said:

Today

- Drink your coffee
- Stay focused and positive
- Don't freak out
- Remember, stabbing people is wrong!
- Are you wearing pants?

I laughed, but this is only funny because I need to have these reminders.

We are living through times of breakdown and breakthrough. It's disorienting and confusing. An old world ordered by continuity, uniformity, and repeatability is dying away, and a new world, ordered by discontinuity, simultaneity, and multiple associations, is emerging. We must harness the capacity to live in between them, to bridge the span between what was and what can be.

How do we do this? Sociologist Margaret Wheatley says in her book, *Turning to One Another*:

> Sacred experiences give us what we need to live in this strange yet wondrous time. We need as many sacred moments as we can find. We invite these moments when we open to life and to each other. In those grace-filled moments of greeting, we know we're part of all this, and that it's all right.

Maybe she's pointing to the real crisis. We are feeling stressed. But we are also lonely. Perhaps we need to be reminded that God made us for each other. We are only fully human and healthy when we are in community with others. Or, as my chosen grandfather often puts it, "Life is about relationships, and the quality of our lives depends upon the quality of our relationships."

Today, I hope you seek out connections with friends, family and colleagues and celebrate those as God's gift in stressful times. We are all in this together.

Reflection Questions

- Does life feel like it's moving too fast, too slow or just right for your thriving?
- What steps could you take to improve the key relationships in your life?

Come From Away

"Beloved, let us love one another, because love is from God; everyone who loves is born of God and knows God." (1 John 4:7)

• • •

For those of us working and playing in aviation, the musical *Come From Away* is a uniquely beautiful story of kindness, sacrifice and community. It is based on the true story of American Airlines Captain Beverly Bass and her experience flying a plane of 158 passengers from Paris, France, to Dallas, Texas, on September 11, 2001. It is worth noting that Captain Bass is famous in her own right, for being the third woman hired as a pilot at American Airlines and the first to make captain—at age thirty-four.

On that day, she had a normal takeoff and was flying over the middle of the Atlantic Ocean bound for Dallas, when she heard over the air-to-air radio that a plane had hit the World Trade Towers. She assumed that it was a small plane, which was bad enough, but it wouldn't be a problem for her flight. Then another pilot announced that a second plane hit the towers, and it was an American 737. At that point, she and her copilot began planning a diversion.

In a matter of minutes, the New York airspace was closed, followed by all US airspace, forcing over 4,000 international flights in the air at that moment to find new places to land. Air traffic control told Captain Bass to expect to land in Gander, Canada.

The airport in Gander was built for service during World War II and afterward, rarely saw major traffic. Within a span of less than twelve hours on September 11, 2001, 38 international aircraft and almost 7,000 people landed in Gander, nearly doubling the size of its population.

When it became clear that the "plane people" were going to be stranded for a few days, the community sprang into action. They housed people in their own homes, cooked every meal, turned the local hockey rink into a freezer for food storage, set up additional phone towers so that people could call home, and cared for the nineteen animals stranded on the planes for those days. The people of Gander showed extraordinary hospitality on one of the hardest days in our shared history.

Recently I was talking with the pastor who was in Gander during that experience. She told me about how the community leaders issued a call for citizens to bring any blankets they could spare to the overflow shelters to keep people warm. All most people had in their homes were handmade quilts, heirlooms they had inherited over generations or created for future ones. Without hesitation, the citizens of Gander brought those quilts to keep the "plane people" warm.

Five days later, on September 16, the FAA opened the US airspace and Captain Bass received word that they were cleared to continue to Dallas. As the passengers packed up and prepared to reboard their planes, the people of Gander who had donated the quilts told the "plane people" to keep them, to take them with them as a remembrance of their meeting and sign of their care. Late in the evening on September 16, the 158 passengers of Flight 49 finally made it to Dallas.

Here is what I love most about this story: Today, throughout the world, beautifully stitched and lovingly gifted quilts are all over the world still keeping people warm. They remind us all that in the end, we are held together, stitch by stitch, through sacred and sacrificial love.

Reflection Questions

- Reflect on a time when your act of hospitality gifted you as much as the other person. What did you learn from that experience?

- Think of all the gifts you have received from others. What do they represent to you?

In Prayer

Sacred Spirit,

In days of hope and grief,
suffering and surrender,
we open ourselves for
healing to break through.

In the face of calls,
for unity and division,
we seek the Ways of Wisdom
to guide us anew.

Be with us, O God,
now and in the days to come,
as we strive in faith
that your will be done.

Amen.

My Racism Was Showing

Thieves must give up stealing; rather let them labor and work honestly with their own hands, so as to have something to share with the needy. (Ephesians 4:28)

• • •

I recently spoke to a group in Canada about this transitional moment in human history. At the beginning of the session, the people in the group went around and offered introductions. Like you, I have sat through what seems like hours of introductions in thousands of meetings. While they are usually interesting, they are rarely teachable moments.

Not this time.

This time, as people were called upon to introduce themselves, they told us their names, where they served, and then what ancestral land they were calling in from. It went something like, "I am Jim. I serve as the regional executive, and I am joining this call today from the ancestral and stolen land of the Tlignit people, today known as British Columbia."

I listened to their introductions with such gratitude for the naming of these forgotten and dismissed stories until I realized I wasn't certain whose ancestral land I was living upon. I have lived much of my life not thinking about the history of the land that has sheltered, fed, and shaped me or the tribes and people who had cared for it.

I have not been in a meeting in the United States where people honored this part of our shared history in their introductions. Now I wonder why. Naming our past—what was stolen, what was forgotten—allows us to be honest about the harm we have caused and the stories we have lost and must now regain.

I also learned another important lesson: While I work every day to become more anti-racist, I have a long way to go in that journey. The life experiences that have shaped me have created a biased lens filled with blind spots. I don't mean harm, but my not knowing, my insensitivity, can create pain both by accident and on purpose. I've now learned that when that happens, I offer an apology, learn from the mistake, and try again. I write this wondering if this is true for you as well.

Being in community with one another in all of our diversity is messy, but so much more beautiful than we could have imagined. We all have much to learn. I give thanks this day that so many of us are committed to trying, realizing that the only way to build a peaceful and equitable world is to do the hard and beautiful work of story-listening and storytelling together.

Oh, and I am writing this from the stolen ancestral home of the Muscogee Nation forcibly removed from their land as a part of the Trail of Tears. Today we call this land Atlanta.

Reflection Questions

- What is the history of the land on which you live?

- Reflect on an experience when you realized your bias blind spot. How did that change you?

In Pursuit of Aliveness

And the one who was seated on the throne said, "See, I am making all things new." Also he said, "Write this, for these words are trustworthy and true." (Revelation 21:5)

• • •

What is the future of spirituality?

I've thought a great deal about this question over many years. I've watched institutional religion decline over my twenty years of being a pastor. I have interviewed hundreds of people about their relationship to those institutions and how they have shifted.

Ultimately, here is what I can say with conviction about the future of spirituality: It will be in service to the pursuit of aliveness.

Scholar and teacher Joseph Campbell reflected in *The Power of Myth*,

> People say that what we're all seeking is a meaning for life. I don't think that's what we're really seeking. I think that what we're seeking is an experience of being alive, so that our life experiences on the purely physical plane will have resonances with our own innermost being and reality, so that we actually feel the rapture of being alive.

Spirituality in its purest essence removes the veil between our inner world and our interdependence with the rest of creation. We glimpse the awe and wonder of being, living within such a glorious universe animated by a loving God. We revel in the Oneness of it all.

Spirituality—the experience of encountering the sacred—may very well be breaking free from congregations as its natural home. Our seeking of the Spirit leads us beyond the structures of most traditional religious spaces and into places that hold more of us—more diversity, more honesty, more brokenness, more joy, more adventures, more questions, more hope.

My advice is to follow the leading of the Spirit even if it means we lose the comfort of what was. All wisdom traditions promise that we find our way to new life through wandering in the wilderness. The wandering leads to wondering, which finally leads to awe. That's the journey of a sacred life, which is the point of it all.

Reflection Questions

- What do you think about Joseph Campbell's observation that we are seeking the experience of being alive?

- How has your faith played a role in that pursuit?

Say What You Wish to See

Let the words of my mouth and the meditation of my heart be acceptable to you, O Lord, my rock and my redeemer. (Psalm 19:14)

• • •

Have you ever wondered why we created the world we have and if there is a better way to develop social structures that serve the common good?

I'm discovering that part of the challenge is our language. We speak—and therefore think—in binaries: immigrant or citizen, black or white, good or bad, rich or poor, male or female. When we think in this way, we create an artificial sense that we must choose to be one or the other. Ultimately, we must value one over the other.

The minute we place a value on one over the other, we create a domination mindset where I want to win, and you need to lose. My power comes from force—from being better/stronger/safer/smarter than you. We can tell the story of much of human history through this simple lens.

I find it all so exhausting. I also find it insane. Literally. This way of relating to one another makes us insane because it forces us into a form of relating that is incongruent with our sacred design. When asked about the essential teaching of faith, Jesus told his disciples, "Love your neighbor as yourself." At the core of us, we are wired for compassion, love, empathy, and care for one another.

Riane Eisler is a Holocaust survivor who went on to become a researcher, author, and activist. She founded The Center for Partnership Systems, where she and her team explore how we might create systems that are more aligned with human thriving.

She challenges our unconscious use of dominating language, suggesting,

— Instead of saying "Fight injustice," say "Heal injustice."

— Instead of saying "Killing time," say "Filling time."

— Instead of saying "Killing two birds with one stone," say "Birthing two birds from one egg."

— Instead of saying "I really crushed it," say "I really brought it to life."

These are little correctives. Until I saw this list, I didn't see how I created a world through my words that undermined my deepest held values.

We speak our world into existence. As we dream of a more just world for all, perhaps the starting place is speaking of peace, love, grace, and healing. What we say determines what we will see.

Reflection Questions

- Can you think of a phrase you casually use that reinforces domination values?

- How do you understand God in relationship to power?

In Prayer

In a culture where punishment and vindictiveness
are substitutes for justice,
and safety is sought through surveillance and security,
may we be creative and courageous in community.
Holding each other accountable for harm,
welcoming the accountability of others,
and accompanying one another with truth and grace,
we turn from domination and control
toward love that protects and transforms.
With assurance of God's steadfast companionship,
may it be so among us.

Amen.

The Art of Visiting

For this is the message you have heard from the beginning, that we should love one another. (1 John 3:11)

• • •

On a recent trip to spend time with family, we practiced the lost art of visiting. We would get up in the morning, fix coffee, and sit on their back porch in comfortable chairs with magazines in our lap (a book in mine). We would talk for a little while, sit in silence for a little while, and then talk again and then silence again. We passed whole days this way, simply being together and enjoying one another's presence and company.

When I think back to my life before the pandemic, I remember myself as so busy with work that I am reasonably sure I would not have allowed myself this time of simply being. I might have been physically present, but my mind would have been racing with all the things to do, emails to return, new ideas to generate. How much of life did I miss, I wonder?

Today, after the isolation we've been through, "visiting" seems like such a beautiful and simple gift. Visiting with those who have shaped us means sitting with a longer timeline of ancestors, past and present, who remind us that it is our connection to one another that matters in the end.

In his book, *Living Philosophies*, Albert Einstein notes,

> Strange is our situation here upon earth. Each of us comes for a short visit, not knowing why, yet sometimes seeming to a divine purpose. From the standpoint of daily life, however, there is one thing we do know: That we are here for the sake of other people—above all for those upon whose smile and well-being our own happiness depends, for the countless unknown souls with whose fate we are connected by a bond of

> sympathy. Many times a day, I realize how much my outer and inner life is built upon the labors of people, both living and dead, and how earnestly I must exert myself in order to give in return as much as I have received and am still receiving.

I have always believed that we are designed by God for one another. 1 John 3:11 reminds us, "For this is the message you have heard from the beginning, that we should love one another." Our seeing one another, knowing one another, caring for one another, and loving one another is THE point of life. The rest is entertainment.

If you have the chance to visit with someone today, I hope you say yes. It's gracious to show up for what matters in the end.

Reflection Questions

- Who would you enjoy visiting with this week?
- How might focusing on being more and doing less help you enjoy what matters most?

Lessons From a Peacemaker

For I, the Lord your God, hold your right hand; it is I who say to you, "Do not fear, I will help you." (Isaiah 41:13)

• • •

Our world is roiling with movements of people longing to be seen, heard, and treated with respect. Every one of us holds this as our deepest need after the need for food and shelter. Our desire to belong to one another in peaceful community is embedded deeply within the soul of each of us as a sacred being. As scriptures teach us, we are each other's keepers.

The challenge is that in so many of our systems, we feel silenced, invisible, and disrespected. Over time we become activists in the cause for recognition and space for our own thriving. When we truly embrace the activist work, we take on the struggle for others—for the common good. We understand that our struggles are interconnected, our pain and joy shared as One.

In 2012, late Congressman John Lewis published *Across That Bridge: A Vision for a Change in the Future of America.* The consummate storyteller and wisdom-bearer, he writes of his experience in the 1960s teaching the rest of us lessons gained over generations for the sake of the world we will create together. He writes,

> *They threw everything at us in the '60s in an attempt to deny the validity of our reality. They called us Communists and hippies, outside agitators and troublemakers. They infiltrated us and investigated us. They floated false rumors and negative propaganda. They ran us down with horses and bludgeoned us with Billy clubs and baseball bats. They jailed us, they beat us, they bombed us, and sprayed us with teargas and fire hoses. They even assassinated a president, a candidate, and a King. President John F Kennedy, Robert Kennedy, and Martin Luther King Jr. were three symbols of hope. They were three men, three leaders who were sensitive to the truth.*

> *Those two brothers began their term as President and Attorney General without a real understanding of the problems of race in the South. But through the protest and the demonstrations, they came to understand how deeply we suffered. They began to hear the mandate to address the very hypocrisy Dr. King spoke about. These men grew. They changed because of what they experienced, and that is all you can ask of another person. Don't close your eyes because you're afraid of what you will see. Be honest in your assessment. Transformation and revelation require an adjustment from what we know to what we know can be.*

Congressman Lewis's words speak to all of us, reminding us of the ongoing struggle to build the beloved community. We mustn't give up on each other, nor accept any less than justice and equity for all.

Reflection Questions

- In what ways are you an activist for the common good?
- What does Congressman Lewis's story teach you about hope for a just and equitable future for all?

Our Collective Dark Night

> *We are afflicted in every way, but not crushed; perplexed, but not driven to despair; persecuted, but not forsaken; struck down, but not destroyed; always carrying in the body the death of Jesus, so that the life of Jesus may also be made visible in our bodies. (2 Corinthians 4:8-10)*

• • •

It seems like we have lived five years in the last seven days. Between witnessing the trauma and heartbreak of violence around the world and living through the fear and foreboding of hurricanes, droughts, fires, and floods, we are staring starkly into the face of the world from our nightmares.

Lately, I've been meditating on "dark night of the soul" experiences. Today, when most of us use that phrase, we casually refer to a challenging moment or a season of sadness. The phrase "dark night of the soul" comes from the Spanish mystic Saint John of the Cross. He writes about the experience as one of profound spiritual transformation marked by a time of purification and clarification of one's senses and then learning to live with radical faith and trust. When you experience a dark night of the soul, you are never the same.

I do have the sense that we are all living through a collective "dark night" experience. By this, I mean that we are living in unsettling days that offer no obvious way "out." We face challenges that do not have easy solutions, leaving us to push past the edge of what is reliable and familiar. These days demand a new imagination from us, one that questions how life works (and doesn't work). Dark nights call for a spiritual response not a therapeutic or purely political one.

Author and psychotherapist Thomas Moore explains in his book *Dark Nights of the Soul: A Guide to Finding Your Way Through Life's Ordeals:*

> The dark night of the soul provides a rest from the hyper-activity of the good times and the strenuous attempts to understand yourself and to get it all right. During the dark night there is no choice but to surrender control, give into

> unknowing, and stop and listen to whatever signals of wisdom might come along. It is a time of enforced retreat and perhaps unwilling withdrawal. The dark night is more than a learning experience; it's a profound initiation into a realm that nothing in the culture, so preoccupied with external concerns and material success, prepares you for.

From this space, the basic question is not "why has this happened" but once tragedy occurs, "who are we now because of it?"

It is there that I think God dwells. It's fair to ask the question, "Where is God?" in this mess of a world we have created. Who are we now? My answer is grounded in two theological understandings. First, I believe that God does not cause bad things to happen. God is not a punitive parent who makes us suffer to teach us lessons. We live in a world of free will, and a condition for that freedom includes suffering.

Second, I understand that God is with us through it all. When we grieve, God grieves, all while hoping for our healing and wholeness. In our "dark nights," I trust God to be bringing resurrection from the crucifying experiences of life. Most often, that transformation comes through the deep, caring love we show one another.

If dark night seasons come in service to profound transformation, then I pray we are seeing the transformation of a world lost to violence, power and greed to one shaped more by compassion and love.

During such times I am reminded again of how much we need each other. Life is not a "do it yourself" project. I am glad that God has created us not for isolation, but for community. When we care about one another and reach out to one another, then we can make it through.

Reflection Questions

- What have you learned about faith in the "dark night" experiences of your life?

- In what ways have "dark night" experiences help you grow as a person?

A Direction Where God Is Not?

Where can I go from your spirit? Or where can I flee from your presence? If I ascend to heaven, you are there; if I make my bed in Sheol, you are there. If I take the wings of the morning and settle at the farthest limits of the sea, even there your hand shall lead me, and your right hand shall hold me fast. (Psalm 139:7-10)

• • •

In a time long ago, a wise old Sufi was making his annual pilgrimage to Mecca. But it was a long walk for him, and the sun was high. Having averaged more than twenty miles a day, once Mecca was in sight, the old Sufi decided to lie down on the side of the road and rest up for his final leg of the journey.

Minutes later, one of the other pilgrims violently kicked his feet. "Get up," he commanded. "You blasphemer, you lie with your feet pointed toward God at the Holy Mosque! What kind of Sufi are you?"

The wise old Sufi cracked one eye open, and said, "I thank you, holy sir. Now, if you would kindly point to a direction where God is not, I will gladly move my feet there."

Once we realize the Oneness of all of life, we are on the path of spiritual awakening. The false lie of life is that we are separate, independent, not connected to one another. The truth is All is One. We are interdependent not just with one another but with all of creation and with God.

Mystic Meister Eckhart said it this way: "The eye through which I see God is the same eye through which God sees me; my eye and God's eye are one eye, one seeing, one knowing, one love." Life becomes radically simple when we finally realize this essential truth.

Saint Teresa of Avila says, "The closer one approaches to God, the simpler one becomes."

Of course, this makes sense. When we give up the illusion of separation and stop playing by the rules we design to control each other, we are free to simply BE.

For today, hold the awareness that God is in you, and you are in God. All is One. Let's see what that reveals to you.

Reflection Questions

- What insights come to you as you meditate on your connection to all of creation?

- What does it mean that God is in you, and you are in God?

In Prayer

Holy One,

whose word is truth
whose will is justice
whose wisdom is peace
whose way is love—
indwell us by thy Spirit
sustain us with grace and
send us on to bless this world freer,
neighbor by neighbor, prayer by prayer.

Amen.

More Beautiful for Having Been Broken

For we are what he has made us, created in Christ Jesus for good works, which God prepared beforehand to be our way of life. (Ephesians 2:10)

• • •

My friend Dana is a sculptor. She creates beautiful, bronzed statues, many of which are on display at some of our national museums and public parks. When she isn't working with bronze, she enjoys working with clay. She makes stunning glazed bowls, plates, and cups, each with their own unique shapes and colors. Her work is breathtaking to behold.

The last time I was in her home, she handed me a bowl that had gold streaks running through what looked to be old cracks. When she saw me looking more closely, she said, "It's called Kintsugi, a Japanese art. This bowl has been through a lot over the years, and it finally broke apart a while ago. But I felt like I could do more with it. So, I melted gold and put it back together."

But then she said something that I will never forget. She said reflectively, "You know, I can now see that it's more beautiful for having been broken."

We can see brokenness everywhere we look. We see gaping cracks in our institutions, our social order, our treatment of the vulnerable among us. We have cracks in our economies, our healthcare systems, our education systems, and clean water sources. The brokenness can feel overwhelming and hopeless.

This is what I know about God. Our God, the Ultimate Potter, looks upon this broken-down world and, just like my friend Dana, sees how it can be more beautiful because of its brokenness, not in spite of it. God never causes the breaks, mind you. But once there, God uses them to bring forth new and even more beautiful creations.

Easter is a story of how God took the brokenness of crucifixion and transformed it into new life through resurrection. God made something new, something even more beautiful in the Risen Christ. We can trust God to do this with us. When everything is off and you feel broken to your core, consider that God is creating within you someone more beautiful for having been broken.

Reflection Questions

- How have you experienced God bringing beauty and love from the broken and painful experiences of your life?
- How can you help others reframe the struggles of their lives as a sculptor reframes broken pieces of clay?

Foolish Daffodils

As for mortals, their days are like grass; they flourish like a flower of the field; for the wind passes over it, and it is gone, and its place knows it no more. But the steadfast love of the Lord is from everlasting to everlasting. (Psalm 103:15-17)

• • •

Thomas (Tommy) Bricker Daughtry was seventy-four years old, still in the prime of his life, when he was diagnosed with lung cancer. He went through the standard treatments—chemo, radiation, shifts in his diet—and it seemed to be working. But in the midst of the pandemic, he went into the hospital for what turned out to be pneumonia. Within a couple of days, they intubated him. He had a series of strokes and passed away on January 15, 2021.

Tommy loved nature. He and his wife Linda retired to the beautiful North Georgia mountains in a home on "Big Creek" where he created a wonderland of gardens, sculptures, bonsai, koi ponds, rock paths, garden sheds, and cedar trees.

In addition to being an artist, professor,. gardener, and all-around Renaissance Man, Tommy also wrote charming little missives that he would post online. I invite us to enjoy a piece he wrote in 2015 and titled "Foolish Daffodils."

> It is thirty-one degrees here this morning at Big Creek. I walked out into the driveway desperately looking for some infinitesimal sigh of the approaching spring of 2015. It is after all the eighth of March.
>
> Of course, there are a few daffodils pushing their green pointy leafy fingers up into the frosty air, but everyone knows that daffodils don't have any sense. They hoist their brilliant yellow tousled heads up into the air without regard for the temperature or timing, trumpeting the approaching spring. They are like overeager children with their enthusiasm overwhelming common sense. You just can't count on the narcissus family for any accurate weather predictions. In the last week or two, I have noticed the crowds of brilliant blond

flowers standing by the Gilmer County roadsides beckoning with false promises. You cannot trust a daffodil!

Many years ago when we lived in Jonesboro a thick patch of King Alfred daffodils stood in the backyard where they bloomed in profusion every spring. One March night during this particular spring, we had a surprising dip in the temperatures. It registered in the low teens, and froze the yellow blooms into stiff immovable statues. The next morning the wind picked up and blew so hard it broke the frozen stems and blooms off at ground level and sent them tumbling end over end down the small hill toward the lake. As they tumbled, the now fragile, brittle flowers broke into hundreds of pieces of bright yellow confetti littering the dry dormant grass in the back yard.

Knowing the shortcomings of daffodils and their unreliability I have to admit this modest plant I like better than most others. Their resurrection every spring gives me assurance and faith in the invisible things that reliably perform with no facilitating from me or anyone else. That enduring speck of unseen life wrapped, housed, and surrounded by layers and layers of the brown sleeping bulb is determined to continue performing as it always has. How I love those daffodils.

Today, take a moment to look at the wonderful gifts that this world offers you, and then hug those you love a bit closer. Life is sacred and precious, over all too soon.

Reflection Questions

- Tommy offers a poetic and entertaining vignette on the determination of the daffodil. What inspiration might the story offer your life?

- Beauty and wisdom are all around us if we take the time to look. Take a moment to notice the tree in your yard, the look on your dog's face, the purple of the flower on your desk. Whatever catches your eye, what might it teach you?

Asking For Help

Ask, and it will be given you; search, and you will find; knock, and the door will be opened for you. (Matthew 7:7)

• • •

A mother posted on our neighborhood app called "Next Door" that she could no longer feed her children or herself. Her reserves had run out. She needed to ask for help.

She wrote: "I am embarrassed to ask this, but I don't have any food to feed my children. I'm not concerned if I don't have food for myself, but I can't do that to them. Can anyone help?"

'Yes," I thought to myself. "In the name of all that is good in this world, yes, we will help."

No one wants to ask their neighbors to help feed their children. I hold deep respect for her courage and vulnerability, as well as anger at the systemic conditions that put her in this position. We must do all we can to help.

Her story is the one that truly tells us who we are as a people and world. Her story, like so many others, holds the fear of not having enough, the courage of asking for help, the vulnerability of being rejected, the pain of unemployment, and the anxiety of having few options to help herself. Her story is the one that has captured God's heart, just as all stories of struggle do.

We don't yet know the ending, but we know that change is coming. She reached out and expressed her need. Will her story be one of a community coming together to help neighbors in need? Will hers be a story of people turning away, afraid that if they help her, they would not have enough for themselves?

During Advent, we prepare for the coming of Emmanuel, God with us. We look for the signs—hope, peace, joy and love. This year, I have my eyes on my neighbor. At the heart of God's inbreaking—how I always know that I am seeing God with us in the world—is when we love one another as ourselves.

Reflection Questions

- What scares you about asking others for help?
- How could we make asking one another for help easier?

The Common Good

All who believed were together and had all things in common; they would sell their possessions and goods and distribute the proceeds to all, as any had need. (Acts 2:44-45)

• • •

In talking about our worrisome descent into self-destruction as a global society, theologian Matthew Fox said, "People in the US spend $56,000 EVERY SECOND on weapons development. I can think of a lot more creative ways to spend that kind of money." Couldn't we all?

Saint Thomas Aquinas, a medieval Roman Catholic scholar, was the first to coin the term "common good." He was concerned about the ways governments care for all people, not just those who have privileges or access to power and wealth. Aquinas noted that when rulers make laws that violate what works for the common good, they become tyrants. Aquinas went on to conclude, "A tyrannical government is not just, because it is directed not to the common good, but to the private good of the ruler."

What does this say about us? Nothing good, I fear.

Instead of building weapons that kill people and destroy our planet, what could we do with $56,000 every second for the common good? We could . . .

- Eradicate hunger
- Build a farm to table movement that supports local community economies
- Develop treatments and vaccines for diseases impacting people around the world
- Give everyone who wants it access to higher education
- Begin the work of reparations
- Provide social services and support to help families thrive
- Rebuild our roads, bridges, and critical infrastructure
- Invest in minority and women-owned enterprises

- Develop clean energy solutions
- Clean our oceans . . .

In other words, we could care for the poor, heal the sick (and our planet), honor our children and elders, and protect the weakest among us. If we refused to invest in greed and tyranny, we could invest in a more just and generous world for all. The core teaching of every major religion says that care for the "common good" is the path to God.

My heart breaks for the hypocrisy of our time. "Good Christians" ignore the teachings of our faith for the sake of greed and selfishness, and somehow still sit unconvicted in pews and wave their Bibles for photo ops. But I cling to the wisdom of American author and Buddhist teacher Joanna Macy who reminds us, "The heart that breaks open can contain the whole universe."

May we all break open for the sake of the common good.

Reflection Questions

- What issues of suffering in the world capture your heart and move you to act?

- Some people think the best way to get through life is to put themselves and their families first. But the Bible says over and over we should care for one another. How does that get expressed in your life?

In Prayer

Beloved,

May you discern wisely
what stories to tell
what stories to receive
what stories to live.

Amen.

The Living Bridges of Meghalaya

One generation shall laud your works to another, and shall declare your mighty acts. (Psalm 145: 4)

• • •

The northeast Indian state of Meghalaya is the wettest region in the world. The Khasi people who have lived there for generations have learned to live with extreme monsoon seasons that bring 32 to 45 feet of rainfall a year. Most of these villages do not have road access and getting from one place to another means crossing wide, dangerous rivers.

Crossing these rivers is impossible without a bridge. But the raging waters presented a profound challenge. Any bridges they built and installed were washed away. Ladders were swept up in the rushing monsoons. They needed a solution that was strong enough to withstand the torrents of water and safely carry them to the other side.

Surrounded by rubber fig trees, the ancient Khasi, in a breathtaking bio-engineering feat, used the aerial roots, nurtured and trained over time, to build living tree bridges. Adventurer Prasenjeet Yadav writes,

> Tree bridges are structures that are literally rooted in the terrain and that thrive under the relentless pressures of the wettest land in the world. After a wait of 10 to 15 years, the trees are old enough to put out aerial roots, which the bridge builders then coax across the river with the help of bamboo scaffolding. This scaffolding doubles as a temporary way for pedestrians to cross the river while the bridge is under construction. Over the years, the aerial roots are pulled and woven to meet the tree on the other side of the river. The roots are tied with one another and eventually they merge by a process of fusion known as anastomosis. Once the tree has reached a certain level of maturity, it adds more roots to the network, which the local people weave into the bridge. After the entire network of roots has sufficiently matured, the bridge reaches a critical strength capable of supporting pedestrians.

Generations of Khasi people have cared for these bridges. They have nurtured roots that they knew they would never walk on, but their grandchildren and great-grandchildren would. They had a vision of bridges that would connect one shore to another, and set out to build them, knowing that it would take more than their generation to finish.

What are we building today that future generations will cherish, giving their lives to continue nurturing and sustaining? I would like to think it was a kinder, more compassionate world woven together by our love for one another and our earth. That is a vision worth inheriting.

Reflection Questions

- What are you building for your life story that you hope future generations will remember?

- How is your life story connected to your ancestors that came before you? What are you carrying forward from them?

In Search of Wisdom

Do not worry about anything, but in everything by prayer and supplication with thanksgiving let your requests be made known to God. And the peace of God, which surpasses all understanding, will guard your hearts and your minds in Christ Jesus. (Philippians 4:6-7)

• • •

With all of the trauma and drama in our lives, I felt I was losing my bearings. So, I wrote a letter to myself. I wrote it as if I were twenty years older than I am today. I imagined my older, wiser self writing to the person I am today, offering advice. I share it with you, not to say "adopt this as your wisdom," but more to say, "if you need to remember who you are, this exercise might help." Try it.

In Search Of . . . Me

Dear One,
You're sad. It's ok.
You're anxious. It's ok.
You're exhausted. It's ok.
You're grieving what used to be. It's ok.
You're worried about what is ahead. It's ok.
Everything you are . . .
You are ok.

You are making hard choices: What in your life will you keep and what will you let go? What in yourself will you keep? What have you outgrown?

This is the work that only you can do. No one is going to save you. No one is going to tell you what to keep of yourself and what to let go. So, take your time. Listen to God's urging. Trust your intuition. You are wiser than you know.

When you are ready, and only when you are ready, prepare for the hardest part. Letting go is the easy part. Creating your new self is the real work. Life and death are things we understand.

> It is what follows—life, death, and life again—that's the part no one wants to endure. It is the new birth. The resurrection. The rising. The awakening. The "you will never be the same again" transformation is the point of it all, but the change we fight the most.
>
> Listen, now. You can sabotage this great work within yourself with a simple thought. You can tell yourself "I'm not worth it." You can tell yourself you are not brave, you are not resilient, you are not lovable, you are not . . .
>
> But you are. You always have been. You just couldn't see it. You are worthy, brave, resilient, and lovable. Every wound, every achievement, every disappointment, every breakthrough . . . all of it brought you here. Now you must learn to see what has been true all along.
>
> Lean in. Be "all in" on this. Commit to your transformation. It won't be easy. Or maybe it will be. But have no doubt, Dear One, it will be worth every single step.

I needed this letter for me, but maybe it will help you too.

Reflection Questions

- Now it's your turn. Write a letter to yourself today from an older, wiser part of you. What would you say?

- How do thoughts like "I can't do this," or "I'm not worth it," get in your way of living a full creative life? Do you let those thoughts stop you or motivate you? How do you want to use those thoughts in your life going forward?

Marking Transitions

> *Do not remember the former things, or consider the things of old. I am about to do a new thing; now it springs forth, do you not perceive it? I will make a way in the wilderness and rivers in the desert. (Isaiah 43:18-19)*

• • •

Sometimes changes in our lives need acknowledgment or ritual. We have lived long enough to accumulate wisdom, experiences, wounds, and redemption, and we need a way to say "Yes! These are the gifts that have brought me this far." Then we can decide whether we want to take them into our future or let them stay in our past, to mark the end of one time and the beginning of something new.

I think about the moment I transitioned from pastoring churches. I loved all that my congregations had taught me. I cherished the memories of baptizing children and visiting elders. I miss writing sermons and leading group studies. I carry the scars of my own leadership missteps and hurt feelings. I give thanks for the lessons I learned and the person I have become because of those years.

When I moved to a full-time focus on consulting with congregations and leaders, I felt I needed to mark that moment of transition. I was different in this role. My work was different. I used journaling as a way of ritualizing the transition. I wrote about my gratitude for all I had gained to that point, and then recognized that my work would be different going forward. I grieved, and I celebrated.

Ritualizing our rites of passage help us integrate the wisdom we have gained and let go of what holds us back. It allows us to hold the grief that comes with change and hold the hope that comes with dreams.

I wonder what rituals we need to hold our grief and our hopes. These are "coming of age" days. We are transforming from one person, community, country, and world into another. We have gained wisdom that we should integrate and celebrate. We have behaviors and ways of being that we need to let go as they no longer serve us.

In these transitions, we give thanks for that world that was. Now, we are different. We sing new songs. We dance new dances. We write new poetry. We pray new prayers. We dream new dreams. God is with us in the flow, doing new things. How shall we mark the shift? How might we tell the story of who we were and who we hope to be?

Reflection Questions

- How might you ritualize the transitions in your life this past year?
- What "new thing" do you sense God is creating in your life?

The Root of It All

They shall be like a tree planted by water, sending out its roots by the stream. It shall not fear when heat comes, and its leaves shall stay green; in the year of drought it is not anxious, and it does not cease to bear fruit. (Jeremiah 17:8)

• • •

Dr. Monica Sharma is a physician and epidemiologist who worked for the United Nations for more than twenty years. She has dedicated much of her life to transformational leadership. In a recent conversation we shared, she said, "In mathematics, the word radical means "root of." It is a way of getting to the base, the root, of a number in its purest form. There is something about human beings, that when we awaken the root of our being, we are capable of creating enormous change."

I've often talked about these days of deep transformation and dislocation as "The Great Unveiling." It is a time of stripping away what has not been working for some time and revealing what is broken in our culture. Dr. Sharma helped me see more clearly that when we get in touch with who we really are, what we value, what we fear, what we hope, then we are being radical. We lead from our rootedness in the ground of Being.

These are essential days. They are undoing us. They are remaking us. They are full of loss. They are full of awakening. They hurt, and they heal. Time spent in these days is messy. It is unpredictable and hard to discern, but we are peeling away what is not essential so that we get to the root. We are on an odyssey of authenticity.

What I can offer as a fellow sojourner is this: Trust the shedding. Trust the process of letting go. Trust that what we create from the "root" of all of us holds the greatest hope for our shared future. A radical is one who gets to the root of the problem and dares to create alternatives to what is not working. We are radicalizing for the common good. I suppose this is what Jesus was dreaming of when he said, "Thy kingdom come. Thy will be done. On earth as in heaven." My deepest prayer is that heaven comes to earth through us.

Reflection Questions

- What has been the hardest part of living through this pandemic? How has it tapped into your roots?
- What is your hope for your own life as you grow new roots in a post-pandemic world?

Coming to Peace

Those conflicts and disputes among you, where do they come from? Do they not come from your cravings that are at war within you? (James 4:1)

• • •

Isa Gucciardi is a psychologist and creator of Depth Hypnosis, a groundbreaking therapeutic model that has won rave reviews from psychotherapeutic and spiritual counselors alike. In her book, *Coming to Peace*, she explores a process for moving through conflict in ourselves, our families and groups based on indigenous practices of honest dialogue and self-reflection. But for any process to work, she says these elements must be present in the people involved:

- Equality – Each person will be given equal time to speak, and every person's experience will be considered of equal value to the experience of every other member of the group.
- Mutual respect – Each person strives to treat other people with respect. This means not interrupting someone when they are speaking and not making negative comments or characterizations.
- Honesty – Each person strives to tell the truth of their experience and be forthcoming about their actions.
- Commitment to personal responsibility – Each person remains fully accountable for their actions and agrees to seriously consider the effects those actions may have had on others.
- Compassion – Each person strives to hold a compassionate space for themself and the other members of the group.
- Tolerance – Each person agrees to practice tolerance even when they do not agree with what is being presented by other members of the group.
- Patience – Each person agrees to practice patience even when they feel upset by what is being presented by other members of the group.

- Willingness to engage – Each person agrees to participate in the process even when things become difficult or when they do not like what is being brought forth.
- Cultivation of inner wisdom – Each person agrees to do their best to attune to their inner wisdom.

I love this list because it's a beautiful encapsulation of a balanced and well-lived life. You show up in your fullest integrity, stay present for one another, act from a place of inner wisdom, and welcome what comes.

Conflict is inevitable in our companies, faith communities, families, and ourselves. James 4:1 says, "Those conflicts and disputes among you, where do they come from? Do they not come from your cravings that are at war within you?"

In some ways, we are hardwired to lose alignment with ourselves and others. To find our way back, we start with ourselves. We take responsibility for our lives—a radical act itself. Then we set about to live from a place of deep intention and fierce honesty.

The more we do this, Gucciardi says, the more we come to peace.

Reflection Questions

- What has conflict taught you about coming to peace within yourself?
- What is scary about taking responsibility for your actions and your life?

Unreliable Winds

Look at the birds of the air; they neither sow nor reap nor gather into barns, and yet your heavenly Father feeds them. Are you not of more value than they? And can any of you by worrying add a single hour to your span of life? (Matthew 6:26-27)

• • •

In general aviation, when a pilot is approaching an airport to land, we are required to listen to a field-specific frequency to get the weather report (ATIS). It will often sound something like this:

Peachtree-Dekalb Tower information X-Ray, 0754 zulu.
Wind zero-eight-zero at eight
Visibility one-zero, light rain
Ceiling 2500 broken, 4500 overcast
Temperature four, dew point one
Altimeter three-zero-zero-three
ILS runway one and ILS runway seven approaches
are in use
Clearance delivery is 119.25
Ground control is combined with tower on 128.4
Advise on initial contact you have information X-Ray

All of the information in an ATIS report is helpful, but there are two critical pieces that a pilot is listening for: the altimeter setting and the wind direction/speed. The altimeter setting allows us to accurately measure the distance between the ground and the airplane. The wind direction and speed tell us which runway we should use. We always want to land INTO the wind. Landing with the tailwind, you risk floating off the runway, something we want to avoid.

As I was completing a flight and coming in to land, I switched over to the airport frequency and listened carefully for these pieces of information. The altimeter setting was 30.06 and the winds were "unreliable."

I chuckled, thinking if that wasn't a metaphor for our time, I don't know what is. These days feel as though we are all flying in unreliable winds. We're being blown in all kinds of directions that feel scary and disorienting. We are trying to land safely, but the forces of politics, power and change are making our journeys feel dangerous. Our natural instincts are to cling to control. We tighten our hands on the yoke of what brings us security—our jobs, family and money. We think, "It's up to me to see us safely through. I better be in command."

But that is exactly the **wrong thing to do**.

When good pilots encounter turbulence, they LOOSEN their grip on the yoke. They trust that the plane is designed to fly, adjusting to the wind to maintain steady, stable flight. If the pilot grips the yoke tightly, it makes the plane less able to adapt. It increases the risk to the flight.

Instead, in the greatest turbulence, you learn to "fly loose." Holding the yoke gently between your fingers, you let the plane do what it was designed to do—fly straight and level. You may need to make corrections to help increase stability but trying to control the plane reduces the flexibility it needs to fly as safely as possible.

We are flying in unreliable winds these days. So, lighten your grip and see if your life begins to fly more smoothy.

Reflection Questions

- What situation in your life might get better if you "loosen your grip" on your need for control?
- What are you learning about yourself and your faith as you live in unreliable times?

In Prayer

God of Grace,
In every season,
In every moment,
May I find your presence
calling me
more fully into myself.
Remembering,
I am your beloved child.
You are waiting for me. Always.

Amen.

Group Discussion Guide

The ritual practice of prayer and contemplation is just as important as the intellectual stimulation of discussion within a group experience. If you wish to use this book as a guide for small groups, I would encourage you to build practices and rituals around the meditations to enrich your experience.

The flow of your time together might look as follows:

Welcome (5 min)

Centering Prayer (2 min)

Scripture Reading (5 min)

Time of Silence (2 min)

Meditation Reading (6-8 min)

Discussion (30 min)

Closing Prayer or Practice (5 min)

All of this could flow within an hour to an hour and a half with attentive facilitation. I encourage you to be creative with the time. If so moved, write prayers and create rituals unique to your group and the reality of the time in which we are living. If that feels overwhelming, I have included suggested liturgies that you can also use to get started.

Welcome

Take special care to create a warm and welcoming feeling as people are gathering, whether in person or online. You might start by saying:

"My name is _______, and I want to welcome you all to this small group. It means a great deal to all of us to pause the frenzy of life and spend this time together. Thank you for being here. We want this to be a community of friends who support one another, grow with one another, and learn from one another. Our goal ultimately is that we become more loving, kind, and compassionate as we follow the ways and teachings of Jesus. Let us begin."

Centering Prayer

Over the course of many weeks, you can explore different types of prayer including prayers of thanksgiving, intercession, confession, and contemplation. Again, be creative as you open yourself to the inbreaking of the Spirit.

Here is a prayer that you could use:

> *Holy One, you created us in your image, to be co-creators, healers, teachers, lovers, prophets, activists, and agitators. Help us to trust your call to us and your presence with us. Guide us this day to bring forth a more just and generous world for all. Amen.*

Or another:

> *Gentle Spirit, come and awaken our longings. Provoke our imaginations. Open our creativity and free our minds. Where we cling to certainty and familiarity, loosen our grip of control. Invite us into the free flow of trusting love as we seek the ways of Jesus. Amen.*

Scripture Reading

Most scripture is beautiful when read aloud and with emotion. To do this well, invite whoever is reading the passage to become familiar with it before you gather to practice the places where inflection and emphasis make the text come to life. They might also memorize the text, especially if it's a single verse, so that the transition flows.

You can move from the Centering Prayer to the scripture reading with words such as:

> ONE: The spirit of God is with us!
>
> **ALL: And with all of creation!**
>
> ONE: Hear now a reading from the book of ______. May these words illuminate the path of love and compassion for ourselves, our neighbors, and the world.
>
> *Read the Passage*
>
> ONE: Receive these words of inspiration!
>
> **ALL: Thanks be to God!**

Time of Silence

After the conclusion of the reading, invite everyone to take one minute (literally, at least sixty seconds) of silent reflection as they sit with the words just spoken. This allows for a deepening of the insights gained as you each consider the wisdom of the scriptures.

At the end of the Time of Silence, you might say something like "For the gifts of quiet insight, we give you thanks. Amen."

Meditation Reading

The meditation for the day can be read aloud by one person, or a couple of people could trade off reading if the selection is longer. It should be read with feeling and energy, not monotony or boredom.

After the meditation is read, you should introduce the time of discussion and engagement.

Discussion

Discussion within a group can sometimes be challenging. Often it helps to establish guidelines for group interaction that ensure the most generative and welcoming space possible. If the group is new or has newly joined members, you might want to review some group discussion guidelines before opening the discussion time. These should include the practices of mutual participation, respect, silence, understanding, and brevity.

To open the discussion, you could use one of the following prompts:

1. What one thought or idea from the scripture or meditation especially intrigued, challenged, encouraged, helped, or surprised you?
2. Share a story about . . .
3. How do you respond to . . .
4. What might you do as a response to . . .

As you hold the space for discussion, try to affirm those contributing and look for ways to deepen the exploration through follow-up questions. Stay in search of wisdom.

When the time is up or the discussion seems to come to a close, end the discussion with the closing prayer or practice.

Closing Prayer or Practice

How you end your time together may be the most creative moment of your experience, and the options for doing so are seemingly endless. You might use the same closing every time, which lends the group a sense of stability. You might close with a song, a poem, body movements like prayer hands, or a simple prayer. Some groups close their time by asking each member to name one word that describes how they are feeling, what they are taking with them from their time together, or what they might need for themselves.

You could say something like:

> *Surely God is with us and goes with us now. Enriched by this gathering, may we act justly, love mercifully, and walk humbly with God.*

You could also invite the group to write its own benediction that you say at the close of each gathering. Here is one that my church group uses:

> *Our time is ending so now our service begins. We leave knowing we are children of God, loved relentlessly. Our promise is to live passionately, love faithfully, and celebrate every moment from now until the finale, for the God of endless grace goes with us. Amen.*

About the Author

Rev. Cameron Trimble is a pastor and denominational leader in the United Church of Christ, an organizational consultant, a frequent keynoter on national speaking circuits, a pilot, and an author of a number of books about faith and leadership. She writes an (almost) daily meditation you can find at www.pilotingfaith.org. She also serves as the CEO of Convergence Network (www.convergenceus.org). For more, see www.camerontrimble.com.

Public contact information:
facebook.com/cameron.trimble
twitter.com/cambtrim
linkedin.com/in/camerontrimble